Thomas Lester, his Lace and the
East Midlands Industry
1820-1905

Thomas (Thomazin) Lester,
1791–1867, c. 1860.

Thomas Lester, his Lace and the East Midlands Industry 1820–1905

ANNE BUCK

RUTH BEAN

CARLTON · BEDFORD

1981

Published by Ruth Bean, Victoria Farmhouse, Carlton, Bedford MK43 7LP, England. Distributed in the USA and Canada by Robin & Russ Handweavers, 533 North Adams Street, Mcminnville, Oregon 97128, USA.

ISBN 0 903585 09 X
Reprinted 1982

Design, James Butler, Saffron Walden
Typesetting, Ken Verow, Wellingborough
Plate negatives, Planwell, Northampton
Printed in Great Britain at the University Press, Cambridge.

Contents

List of Illustrations   vii

Foreword   ix

1 The East Midlands Lace Industry at the Beginning of the Nineteenth Century   1

The Lace Merchants   3
The Lacemakers   3

2 Thomas Lester and Sons — the First Phase 1820—50   6

Thomas Lester 1791—1867   6
Problems of the Lace Manufacturers   6
Problems of the Lacemakers   9
The Lacemakers' Craft   10

3 Thomas Lester and his Lace 1850—70   14

The Lester Collections   15
The Great Exhibition 1851 and After   39
The Lester Lace   41
Lace Manufacturers and the Children of the Industry   72

4 The Second Generation 1870—1909   87

The End of the Lace Schools   90
The Lace Associations   99
The Last Years   101

References   103

Select Bibliography   106

Index   107

List of Illustrations

1	Trade card of Thomas Lester, c. 1840	15
2	Page from album of lace samples, 1800—50, originally the account books of the surveyors of the highways, Olney, Bucks.	17
3	Page from album of lace samples, John Spencer, Wellingborough, 1850—80; borders 1820—40	18
4	Page from album of lace samples; insertions, 1800—50	19
5	Part of page from album of lace samples; borders, 1830—50	20
6	Two pages of an exercise book of pencil drawings for lace, 1830—50	21
7	Lace drafts, dated 1846	23
8	Drafts for point ground lace, 'Lester'	22
9	Draft for point ground lace, 1841	24
10	Draft for handkerchief border, point ground lace, 1840—60	25
11	Draft for handkerchief border, point ground lace, 1840—60	26
12	Draft for handkerchief border, 1855—70	27
13	Parchment pattern for cap, point ground, 1840—60	28
14	Lacebuyer's work book, 1827	29
15	Drafts for lace, 1855—7, 'Lester'	30
16	Drafts for lace, 1857, 'Lester'	31
17	Border, fruiting vine design, 1860—80	32
18	Draft for Plate 17	33
19	Draft for border, convolvulus design, 1860—80	36
20	Flounce, convolvulus design, 1860—80	34
21	Draft for handkerchief border, convolvulus and fern design, 1860—80	46
22	Corner of handkerchief border, convolvulus and fern design, 1860—80	47
23	Handkerchief, border in convolvulus and fern design, 1860—80	45
24	Draft for handkerchief border, rose and thistle design, 1860—80	48
25	Corner of handkerchief border, rose and thistle design, 1860—80	49
26	Handkerchief border, rose and thistle design, 1860—80	50
27	Border, rose and thistle design, 1860—80	51
28	Border, rose and thistle design, variant of Plate 27	51
29	Headpiece of cap, rose and water lily design, 1860—80	52
30	Cap, rose and water lily design, as worn	54
31	Collar and cuffs, cornucopia design, 1860—90	55
32	Cuffs, eagle design, 1860—80	56
33	Cap lappets, ostrich design, 1860—80	58
34	Headpiece of cap, ostrich design, 1860—80	60
35	Cap, ostrich design	62

36	Handkerchief, Honiton lace border in fern design, 1862—4	64
37	Brocaded silk, 1851	65
38	Cap, convolvulus and fern design, 1860—80	66
39	Cap, convolvulus and fern design, as worn	68
40	Borders, rose and leaf design, in raised work, 1860—80	77
41	Collar with corded trail, priced 10/—, 1850—80	78
42	French designs for borders, 1850—70	79
43	Part of parchment pattern for a bonnet veil, 1855—70	80
44	Deep collar with plaited ground, 1850—70	81
45	Figured silk, convolvulus design, 1847—9	82
46	Collar and cuffs, leaf design, 1860—80	83
47	Collar, 1860—80	84
48	Border with crenellated trail, 1860—80	85
49	a Shop of C. and T. Lester, 115 High Street, Bedford, c. 1890	91
	b The site today, now occupied by the Midland Bank Ltd	91
50	a Thomas James Lester, 1834—1909, c. 1900	92
	b Trade card of C. and T. Lester, c. 1895—1900	92
51	Collar, rose design, 1893	93
52	Collar, flower leaf and berry design, 1893	94
53	Collar, acorn design, 1880—1900	96
54	Collar with corded trail, 1880—1900	97

Acknowledgements

Plates 1, 2, 6, 7, 10—12, 17—35, 38—41, 44, 46—48, 49a, 50a—b, 51—54 by courtesy of the Cecil Higgins Art Gallery, Bedford.
Plates 3—5, 8, 9, 13—16, 42, 43 by courtesy of the Luton Museum, Bedfordshire.
Plates 36, 37 by courtesy of the Victoria and Albert Museum, London.
Plate 45 by courtesy of Manchester City Art Galleries.
Plate 49b by courtesy of the Midland Bank Ltd, Bedford.

Foreword

The idea of a book based on a collection of lace now in the Cecil Higgins Art Gallery, Bedford, arose from the interest shown in this lace by practising lacemakers who, in the last few years, have revived what was once a local cottage industry as a craft of leisure. The collection was bequeathed to the town of Bedford in 1945 by Miss Amy Lester. She was the daughter of Thomas James Lester, the last member of a family who had been in business as lace dealers in Bedford from the 1820s to 1905.

At first the plan was to discuss the lace, its designs and techniques, in relation to the lace of its time, and also in the context of the Lester business; the business of a dealer in hand-made lace during the period which saw the final decline of an industry which had existed in the East Midlands since the late sixteenth century. Closer study revealed the first major difficulty: the lace had been preserved but not recorded and none of it was dated or confirmed by any external evidence. The second difficulty, that there were no records of the Lester business preserved with the collection, was obvious from the outset, but this I hoped might be overcome by further search. The results of this search have been disappointing and it has not been possible to compile a full account of the working of this particular business; a business which was maintained by two generations of the Lester family, the founder, Thomas Lester, who died in 1867, and his two sons, Charles Fox and Thomas James.

So it has been necessary to widen the field and to give a more general account of the lace dealers and the organisation of the industry in the East Midlands, from contemporary sources, as a background for Thomas Lester and his lace. Here, for once, we have Thomas Lester's own words, when he speaks for the industry, giving evidence to the Children's Employment Commission of 1862. Recollections of working for Charles and Thomas Lester were gathered mainly in the 1940s when I first began to work on the history of the industry. I was then able to speak to lacemakers whose memories went back to the late 1860s, the 1870s and 1880s.

My debt to those who helped me in preparing this book goes back to this time, and I should like to acknowledge the help of all those who spoke to me of their experience as lacemakers in the declining years of the industry. I also had the privilege then of working with the late Miss C. C. Channer who not only taught me how to make lace and shared with me a knowledge of lace and lacemaking acquired over many years, but also shared her experience of working with the lacemakers of the last years of the nineteenth century and early years of the twentieth century, taking recollection a generation further back. I am glad to have this opportunity to acknowledge also the help I had at this time from Dr J. G. Dony, author of *A History of the Straw Hat Industry,* and Miss J. Godber, then county archivist.

ix

At every stage of the book I have had the most generous co-operation from Miss Halina Grubert, curator of the Cecil Higgins Art Gallery. I am most grateful to her for her interest and enthusiasm and for her ready help at all times, and also for the kindness and help I always received from the staff at the Gallery. I owe much to Miss Margaret Greenshields who was curator of the Gallery when the Lester collection was handed over to it. Without her initial work on it and the work of Miss Ann Balfour Paul, former assistant at the Gallery, my task would have been much more difficult. I should like to acknowledge the help I have had from Mr J. Turner, Bedford Museum; Mrs D. Fudge and Mrs Marian Nichols, Luton Museum; Miss J. Hodgkinson, Northampton Museum; and Aylesbury Museum; Miss Patricia Bell, county archivist, and the staff of the County Record Office, particularly Mr James Collett White. My thanks also go to Miss Santina Levey, Keeper of Textiles, Victoria and Albert Museum, who not only gave me help in my searches in the collection there, but was kind enough to read the manuscript; and to Mrs Eunice Arnold for her comments. I am grateful to my brother and sister-in-law who read both text and proofs for me; and to my niece, Mrs Elizabeth Bentley, for her typing of the manuscript.

It will be obvious that the text is only part of the book and that it owes much to the skilful photography of Mr Robert Irons who took the photographs of items in the Luton Museum (Pls 3-5, 8, 13, 15, 16, 42, 43) and Mr Miles Birch who was responsible for all the photographs of the Lester collection at the Cecil Higgins Art Gallery. My final thanks are to Mrs Ruth Bean for her understanding and encouragement and the meticulous care she has given to every detail of the production of this book.

Anne Buck, March 1981

1 The East Midlands Lace Industry at the Beginning of the Nineteenth Century

The English bobbin lace industry became established during the seventeenth century in two main areas; in the south-west in Devon, and in the East Midlands counties of Bedfordshire, Buckinghamshire and Northamptonshire. The technique used differs in the two areas. In Devonshire lace the pattern is worked first and then, as a separate operation, its different parts are linked together with bars or a mesh ground; this was the method of the Italian bobbin lace of Milan, and of Brussels lace. Lace made in the East Midlands was worked as a continuous fabric in a single operation; the method of the Italian bobbin lace of Genoa and the Flemish laces of Antwerp, Mechlin, Valenciennes and Lille.

The East Midlands industry was coming to the end of its last period of prosperity, when Thomas, or Thomazin, Lester, in the 1820s or a little earlier, became a lace merchant in Bedford. The wars with France from the 1790s had reduced the flow of competing foreign laces and brought improvement in quality as well as quantity, for the manufacturers were able to encourage the making of more expensive laces to take the place of those normally imported. A new scale of duties on foreign lace had been imposed in 1806, a sliding scale with the highest percentage of duty, 30%, falling on lace below 5s a yard.* As this low-priced lace, narrow borders, edgings and insertions, was the chief manufacture of the East Midlands the new duties gave protection to the East Midlands industry. Lace up to 25s a yard was made in the district during the eighteenth century, but an Olney manufacturer stated in 1780, 'Where there is one yard made above Five Shillings there are 1000 made under.'.[1]

The new scale of duties was soon threatened. Even before the end of the war in 1815 there was a proposal to allow all foreign lace to enter under a duty of 20% *ad valorem*, a revision much less favourable to the narrow laces of the East Midlands. The manufacturers of the three counties of Bedfordshire, Buckinghamshire and Northamptonshire formed a committee to fight the proposal and in 1815 presented a petition to Parliament. They succeeded in getting the protection they asked for in 1819 when higher duties were levied, 2s 6d a yard for lace costing up to 5s, 8s 4d for lace of 20s to 25s, and £40 per cent for lace over 25s.[2] This was the greatest protection English lace had received since the repeal of the short-lived act of prohibition in 1699. So in 1820 all seemed well.

The fashions of these years also helped the industry. The fashion in lace at the end of the eighteenth century changed in harmony with the changing character of all textiles and a major change in dress. The stiff contours of mid-eighteenth cen-

*Before 1971, when the UK adopted decimal currency, the pound (£) was divided into 20 shillings (s) and the shilling into 12 pence (d).

tury dress, expressed in heavily patterned, solid silks, were breaking into softer, more flowing lines expressed in light silks and muslins. The new style, a slim, high-waisted dress, emerged in the 1790s and remained with minor changes until 1815, and then in a final phase until 1820.

The texture of lace in the mid-eighteenth century, although fine and delicate, was like the silks, closely patterned. As other fabrics grew lighter in pattern as well as texture, lace became more transparent, by the breaking up of the closely woven intricacy of its patterns into small sprigs scattered over a light, meshed ground. The simplicity of the East Midlands laces was well suited to the new simplicity of dress. Lace was used with the almost universal white muslin of dresses, caps, cloaks and scarves not only as trimming; insertions of lace banded into the muslin were part of the fabric of the garment.

The different lacemaking centres developed characteristic types of mesh for the groundwork of their laces. At the beginning of the nineteenth century the ground chiefly used in the East Midlands was a mesh which had two threads twisted on four sides and crossed on two. This, the lightest mesh of all, was also the mesh of Lille lace. Its French name is *fond simple.* The second ground was an hexagonal mesh of two threads twisted, the sides extended to form six small triangles with another twist of the threads. From this comes its most descriptive English name, *six-pointed star.* It is also known as *kat stitch, wire ground* or *French ground,* although it appeared in eighteenth-century lace from Antwerp and Mechlin, as well as in the French Point de Paris, with the name *fond double.* In the nineteenth century it was also the ground of Chantilly lace and from this gets its other French name *fond chant. Wire ground* seems to have been the term used in the industry in the first half of the nineteenth century and later so I shall keep this name and use the term *point ground* for the Lille mesh, including the wire-grounded laces within it where distinction is irrelevant.

This change in the character of lace, the development of a comparatively large area of uniform mesh was to have a serious effect on the making of lace by hand. The problem of producing lace by machine was lessened when so much of any lace was a plain mesh. A type of net based on the looped technique of the knitting machine had been produced by 1780, but further experiments led to the machine of John Heathcoat, which in 1809 produced a twisted net, very close to the mesh of the Lille and East Midlands lace. At first these nets were used as a fabric for embroidery. Patterns similar to those of contemporary lace were darned in with a needle or worked in chain stitch with a tambour hook. Embroidered net was soon a fashionable fabric for the larger items of dress, veils, scarves and complete dresses worn over underdresses of thin silk. Eugenia Wynne had one of these for her wedding dress in 1806, 'My bridal array consisted of a white satin underdress and a patent net over it, with a long veil.'[3]

At first the narrow laces of the East Midlands industry did not suffer greatly from the new invention. Devonshire lace, with its different technique, made use of the new fabric to develop another type of lace in which hand-made patterns were sewn on to a machine-net ground. Disaster came to the East Midlands when, after much experiment, lace in its entirety was produced on a machine, pattern as well as ground in one operation, by the 1840s. This lace had taken East Midlands work as its model and machine-made lace very closely resembling the contemporary insertions, borders and flounces of the East Midlands, was produced. The long struggle of the industry against the machine-made laces had begun.

The Lace Merchants

The fortunes of the lace industry — in both senses of the word — were in the hands of the lacebuyers or lacemen who, by the nineteenth century, were calling themselves lace merchants, dealers or manufacturers. They were wholesale traders whose way of business was already established at the beginning of the eighteenth century and was described, in one of the many petitions of the industry, in 1717,

'These wholesale men travel weekly to London, where they sell their lace and buy thread and silk, which they bring home and deliver to their workwomen who by their directions work or weave it into several sorts of lace, as their respective masters (the wholesale lacemen) direct, which, when done, the workwomen once every week deliver to their respective masters who pay them what they earn. The wholesale bone-lacemakers every Monday morning go to London with their lace they have caused to be made, where they have two large chambers to sell the same. One of these is the George Inn, Aldersgate Street (the market day being Tuesday), the other is the Bull and Mouth in St Martin's by Aldersgate (the market day being Monday).'[4]

This relationship between lacemakers and lacebuyers continued. The lacemakers were never quite employees for they were not bound to work exclusively for one buyer, only to bring him all the lace made from patterns supplied by him. This was important for the lacebuyer and ultimately for the industry. The buyers were responsible for providing new patterns, reflecting changing fashion and demand. The patterns had to be drawn and then translated into a working draft, the most skilled and difficult part of lacemaking. No lacebuyer would go to the expense of acquiring new designs and drafting new patterns unless he knew that the lace made from them would be exclusive to him. The life of the industry depended on this flow of new expression and a permanent weakness here was an underlying cause of nineteenth century decline.

The wholesale buyers travelled to London with their lace where they sold to specialist lace retailers, and to warehouses which supplied travelling salesmen. They also made journeys to other provincial and fashionable centres, selling to drapers and milliners as well as specialist retailers. But in the lacemaking districts, haberdashers, drapers, milliners, grocers might have a small lace-dealing section of their business, working directly with local lacemakers, either as retailers or as wholesale dealers. R. Griffin of Bedford was described as grocer and lacedealer in 1790. In Harrold, John Coleman, simply described as shopkeeper in directories of 1823 and 1839, took out a licence to deal in lace in 1826, a regulation imposed by the Act of 1806.[5]

The Lacemakers

No one looking at the finest of the lace and lace patterns from the early years of the nineteenth century could doubt that lacemaking was a skilled operation, 'It is an education in lacemaking and design to study and work out the old parchments.'[6] The lacemaker did not, however, enjoy a very high working status. From its earliest appearance in the East Midlands at the end of the sixteenth century lacemaking had been regarded as work for the poor, 'women and children who have no other means of subsistence'.[7] When the lace manufacturers' committee stated in 1815 that the number of workers in the three counties was upwards of 150,000 and that in many of the smallest parishes lace to the amount of £2,000 to £3,000 was made annually, they added, significantly, 'even under these circumstances the Poor are obliged to apply for relief to the Parish'. That skilled workers could produce admired fabrics of some beauty was of less importance than the fact that this domestic industry supplemented the agricultural wages of the men. The combined family earnings produced, at least when lace 'was good', the income needed for bare subsistence.*

In 1800 Arthur Young gave 8d a day as average earnings in lacemaking, 1s for a good worker and 20d a rare achievement. A year later he quoted 4s a week average and 10s a week for a good worker. It is uncertain whether 'good worker' meant a worker of average ability but constant application for long hours, or a highly skilled worker, but it was probably the latter. Not all lacemakers, many of them mothers of young families, were able to work long hours at lace or undertake the more demanding patterns. The best lacemakers, those who worked on lace of 25s a yard would, of course, receive a higher price for their lace, but it took much longer to work any length of it. So, in the end, to what extent greater skill was matched by financial reward is not clear. What is clear is that these skills were not given adequate recognition and incentive to develop nor seen as an asset when competition from the machines threatened. Arthur Young was one of those who defended the lacemakers and their work when, in the war years, the comparative prosperity of a full-time lacemaker excited some disapproval,

'By application and consequent excellence they arrive at a degree of skill which gives them from 1s to 2s a day . . . to abandon all except the main object of their industry is just what we commend in every other pursuit . . . Then why not in this? *But they are so ignorant that they make bad servants, they do not even know how to sweep a room.* So much the better, you would hire one in ten for housemaids. Would you keep nine idle to supply the tenth?'[8]

Children in the lacemaking counties worked side by side with adults. In the seventeenth and eighteenth centuries some were given formal apprenticeships by parents or guardians, and many of the poor by parish overseers who also financed shorter periods of tuition and supplied equipment. In the workhouses of the eighteenth century, children were taught to make lace and their work was then sold by the overseers or the workhouse master to the local lacebuyers. These children are likely to have made only the simplest laces, narrow edgings and insertions.

From the beginning of the nineteenth century there are references to lace schools outside the workhouses. Thomas Batchelor, a farmer at Lidlington, gave an account of them in his *Agricultural View of Bedfordshire,* 1808,

'Children are taught to make lace at about six or seven years old, and they occupy so much of the attention of their school mistress that the expenses of teaching them amounts to 3s a week for a month or six weeks according to their capacity. After they have learned the rudiments of the art their ordinary schooling is 6d a week.'

This account is evidence of the teaching of lacemaking in the schools at this time, even if the tuition period was short. Later references rarely make so great a distinction between the initial, expensive period of tuition and the following, much reduced, weekly charge for supervision. In Chesham, Buckinghamshire, there were

---

* One example from the family budgets quoted by Sir Frederic Eden in *The State of the Poor,* 1797, is that of a Northamptonshire labourer with a wife and five children between one and nine years of age. His earnings were £20 a year with an additional £2 6s for digging graves and ringing the church bell. His wife earned about 6d a week by making lace and the elder children between them about the same amount. The main item of food was bread which cost them 7s to 8s a week. Bread was then rising in price, at 7d for a 2lb loaf, and was to rise still higher. The earnings of mother and children were enough to provide either 2 oz tea and ½ lb sugar, or ½ lb butter and 1 lb beef a week for these seven people. The wages of the agricultural labourer rose only slightly during the nineteenth century and there were times when it fell. In the 1880s many were still earning no more than 10s a week. But there had been a fall in some food prices in the second half of the century. The 4d a day earned by Mrs Dawson (p. 89) would have bought her ¼ lb tea or butter, or ½ lb bacon, or 1 lb sugar.

4

three lace schools in 1819 attended by 40 children who were charged 4d a week in the summer and 5½d in the winter, and young children 'who are just beginning the lacemaking 6d a week throughout the year'. The extra charge in the winter months was for candles.[9] It was reckoned at this time that children, put to school at five, could after two years earn 2s to 2s 6d a week by their lace. From this 4d to 6d a week was deducted for their attendance and 3d or 4d for material.

2 Thomas Lester and Sons – the First Phase 1820-50

Thomas Lester 1791–1867

Thomas or Thomazin Lester, the son of John and Sarah Lester, born Cole, was born in Abington Pigotts, Cambridgeshire in 1791. He first appears in Bedford records in July 1818 when he married Elizabeth Fox at St Pauls Church; both were 'of this parish'.

In 1817 Elizabeth Fox had been received into full communion of the Bunyan Meeting and a year later, after their marriage, 'Brother Leicester' was also received into full communion and Thomazin Lester's long connection with the Bunyan Meeting at Bedford, as well as with the lace industry, had begun.[10]

According to the census of 1821, Thomas Lester was a 'manufacturer' living in the parish of St Peter, Bedford. In the church rate book of 1827 he was assessed for a house rated at £12 and a garden rated at £3. He appears as a lace manufacturer and dealer in Harpur Street in *Pigot's National and Commercial Directory*, 1830–1, which also lists six other dealers in Bedford and, in all, seventy-four lace dealers throughout the three counties, Bedfordshire, Buckinghamshire and Northamptonshire.

The bare facts of Thomas Lester's early career – his baptismal name Thomasin or Thomazin was soon shortened to this more usual form – suggest that, coming to Bedford from a village outside the main lacemaking area, he was not already working in the industry, although his wife, Elizabeth Fox, may well have been a lacemaker. She was probably Elizabeth, daughter of James and Hannah Fox, of St Cuthberts parish, born in 1796. In Bedford about 1820 lace-dealing was an obvious line of business for a young man to embark on and it did not need a great deal of capital to make a start.

Problems of the Lace Manufacturers

During the 1820s fashion was still, intermittently, on the side of the East Midlands lace industry. The lines of dress were changing by 1815 as the hem line swung out from the vertical to a greater width, and ornament increased with frills and flounces at the hem and more trimming on the still short-waisted bodice. The lace of the East Midlands can still be seen in these frills and flounces on surviving dresses of white muslin and on indoor caps which had also grown more elaborate. But at the same time silk bobbin lace, blonde, had become fashionable, particularly for evening wear. This lace was made in France at Chantilly, Caen and Bayeux and, in spite of the name, could be in black as well as cream silk. Although the technique of making this lace was the same, the East Midlands was slow to produce much of this type. The competition of embroidered nets was also having some effect. In 1830 the lace dealers of the three counties again approached the Duke of Buckingham, who had supported them in their petition to Parliament in 1815, with a new petition to forward to Queen Adelaide on account of the falling demand for the white thread lace of the East Midlands. The reason they gave was that it 'had recently been little worn by the nobility and had become unfashionable'. They entreated the Queen whose portraits often show her wearing the lustrous and fashionable blonde, to wear thread lace 'at your coming Drawing Room, or in any way you may think fit you would be pleased to introduce pillow lace again into fashion'. A general promise of help was received from Windsor Castle.[11]

A good deal of thread lace was still being worn, but there was competition not only from blonde lace, which reached its peak of fashion in the 1820s and 1830s, but from embroidered muslin. Embroidered muslin was fashionable for the large collars worn in the 1830s and for the morning caps which were also large and elaborate over hair dressed high on the head. The narrow laces of the East Midlands, edgings and insertions, were used with embroidered as well as plain muslin in the white accessories needed to complete the dress of the time. As the style of dress changed in the 1840s collars and caps became smaller and morning caps were less generally worn, but day dress always had its white collars and cuffs of muslin and lace. Wider laces were used for trimming evening dress, in tiered flounces on the skirt, draped and festooned over it and on the bodice. Some of the high-necked, fitting bodices of the day dresses of the 1840s had a front opening and with these muslin and lace-trimmed chemisettes were worn. When the fitted sleeve of the early 1840s opened out at the wrist in the late 1840s, muslin and net undersleeves were worn; these too might be trimmed with lace. Undersleeves in great variety were a feature of dress from the late 1840s to the 1870s and no day dress with open sleeves was complete without them.

The organisation of the industry still retained its eighteenth-century structure, but there were changes in its working. James Millward, an Olney lace merchant, told the Select Committee on Arts and Manufactures in 1836, 'The manufacturer appoints a day when his "workers" as they are called meet him at an inn and he buys the lace and perhaps gives them new patterns and parchments to work on and sees no more of them until the next journey which may be a month or six weeks afterwards.' Already before the end of the eighteenth century the lacebuyers were decreasing in number and dealing with a larger number of workers, though not all of them full-time lacemakers. In 1780 James Pilgrim, also of Olney, said he employed 800 'hands' whereas at the beginning of the century the lacebuyers spoke of 100, 200 and 300 workers.[12] The interval between each collection of lace and giving out of new work was now much longer, a month or six weeks instead of the earlier weekly visits. This lessened the contact between the buyer and his lacemakers and his control over the work done. James Millward continued,

'The other day . . . a woman brought me a bit of lace. I didn't know but that she had been all the time working for me. I took it. She wanted a new pattern. Some person reminded me that she had not been for a twelve month before, and that when she wanted a new pattern, she came to me again to get one to hawk about and sell as she pleased.'

The practice of lacemakers getting patterns from one dealer and selling the lace to another was not a new one and had always been a problem for a lacebuyer when he invested in new designs. The much longer interval between the buyer's visits now increased the temptation for the lacemakers to sell elsewhere. A month or six weeks was a long time to wait to turn lace into money, especially as times grew harder,

'There are a number of persons . . . collecting anything they can buy and they are searching for every new pattern they can lie their hands on, which they will buy if they can . . . They buy the lace which serves them as a pattern . . . The persons that go about in that way have no patterns of their own; they make their livelihood by purchasing those that have been given by other persons taking them to some manufacturer or dealer and selling them weekly and probably daily; the manufacturer or lace merchant would not do it himself, but will purchase the new pattern of these travelling people; they have sometimes 20 or 30 or 40 in a day with a little box in which they collect the laces.'

A short length of lace was quite enough for one of these dealers who wanted to use it as a pattern only, while the original dealer needed lengths of several yards to sell from his pattern. James Millward acknowledged that certain lacemakers working for him could be trusted with any pattern, but deplored the change amongst the dealers themselves.

'The persons at present engaged in the lace manufactory or rather lace dealing are quite another class from what they were 20 years since. On account of piracy, many persons have left the trade altogether in disgust, and it has been taken up by shopkeepers and travellers and other persons who know very little about it.'

His main plea was for copyright protection of patterns. He was convinced that trade would improve if there were better patterns available and these were protected. He said there was a great scarcity of pattern drawers in the East Midlands industry and was very critical about the standard of pattern drawing, 'There are only two or three persons who draw lace patterns and they do very little. The reason assigned is that it is of no service, because if one person buys the pattern, another person has the lace.' His father, who had 'spent half-a-century in lace dealing and pattern drawing', had taught him. He had specimens of French lace sent to him which he studied and after altering, varying and redrawing, 'dared at last to have a style of my own formed on the French mode and that style has prevailed in the best laces to the present time'.[13] Examples of Millward work can be seen in two drafts, dated 1828 and 1838, reproduced in Thomas Wright's *Romance of the Lace Pillow.* They show East Midlands lace at its best, similar to Lille, yet with its own quality and character.

Like most of the witnesses of the Select Committee James Millward was critical of the lack of encouragement given to the practical application of art to manufacture, especially compared with France and Germany. The Report of the Select Committee was one of the factors which moved the Board of Trade to establish a school of design in London; to be followed during the 1840s by schools in the main manufacturing centres. No fresh vigour seems to have come to the East Midlands from this development, unless indirectly from Nottingham where a Government School of Design was set up in 1846. Mrs Treadwin's shawl of Honiton lace which was shown at the Paris Exhibition of 1867 had its pattern of roses and convolvulus, 'designed by an artist of Nottingham'.[14]

Millward's other recommendation, that lace designs should be protected, had a limited implementation in the Design Act of 1842. Lace designs (class 13) received protection for a year provided they were registered by depositing a copy of the design with the Registrar of Design at the Patent Office. It was, however, the manufacturers of machine-made lace who took advantage of this protection for their designs rather than the dealers in hand-made lace. John Millward and

W. H. Handscomb of Newport Pagnell both registered designs in the 1840s, but the name of Thomas Lester does not appear in the register.[15]

English lace did not long enjoy the protection of the 1819 Act. In 1826 the duty was changed to £30 per cent with no special protection for lower-priced laces, and during the 1840s it was again lowered; in 1842 to £12 10s per cent; in 1846 to £10 per cent. After 1860 all foreign lace was free of duty.[16]

Problems of the Lacemakers

To J. H. Matthiason, whose *Bedford and Its Environs* was published in 1831, lacemaking was still the main manufacture of the town,

'The staple manufacture of Bedford is thread or pillow lace which is still carried on to a considerable extent and occupies nearly all the female population of the working classes, notwithstanding the cheapness and perfection to which machinery has brought the cotton lace . . . . It is however regretted that by this means the industrious poor who were formerly able to earn a comfortable livelihood have been reduced to such a state as to render the most toilsome application insufficient to obtain a bare subsistence.'

The term thread lace, in use since the eighteenth century, distinguished the laces of linen thread from those of silk.

The 1830 petition of the lace manufacturers repeated the figure of 150,000 lacemakers in the three counties, given in the 1815 petition, but James Millward thought this was an over-estimate. The rather unreliable census of 1841 gave a figure of 9,773 which seems unlikely as the return in the 1851 census, when all other evidence is of a decline, was 26,670. Errors and miscalculations were particularly easy for an occupation in which part-time work was general but, allowing for an over-estimate in 1830 and ignoring the 1841 figure, the fall in twenty years to the 1851 figure gives some measure of the decline. It was in the 1840s that the full impact of the competition of Nottingham machine-made lace was felt. By then the machines were producing patterned laces, imitating the patterns of East Midlands lace. All these new laces, narrow borders and edgings, wider borders and flounces, grounded with a net based on the Lille ground, could be sold at much lower prices than the hand-made lace.

In the face of the competition from machine-made lace, two courses were open to the manufacturers of hand-made lace: to concentrate on the finer laces for a limited market, laces whose intricate, non-repetitive patterns could still compete with the machines; or to continue to make the lace which the machines were now copying, trying to produce it more cheaply to compete with machine lace in price. The first of course was hardly practical for the East Midlands industry with its concentration on the cheaper laces of the hand-made market. So, to keep up with the pace of the machines the designs became more repetitive and the lace was worked with less fine thread. This lowered the price and with it the quality; it also blunted the skill of the lacemakers.

In the southern half of Bedfordshire, the industry of straw-plaiting now gave a better living than lacemaking and, where straw-plaiting was available as alternative work many lacemakers took this up instead. It was much easier to become a competent plaiter than a competent lacemaker. In plaiting the trading unit was the score, twenty yards of plait, which in the plainer braids meant about eight hours' work. The price for common plaits in 1837–8 was 1s a score, making average earnings with an eight-hour day 5s to 6s a week. 'Those engaged in plait will earn double the wages of those who make lace.'[17] A good lacemaker might now earn

9

only 3s a week, and weekly earnings of 1s to 2s 6d were more general. Thirty years before the comparable figures had been 10s and 4s. To earn even these reduced amounts the lacemakers had to produce more lace and so work for longer hours. In evidence to the Commission on the Employment of Children in 1843, all the older women agreed that hours had become longer because of the lower price of their lace. Elizabeth Jennings, aged twenty-six, of Stony Stratford told the inspector, 'Trade ain't half so good now as when I began, if a young woman were to sit 12 or 14 hours close work they might earn 6d a day or 3s a week.' She had probably started at about the age of six or seven in 1823—4. Most of the older women had been to lace schools at the beginning of the century. Mrs Ann Freeman of Brackley began lacemaking in her sixth year, 'I went to a school, schools were much the same then as now.' Sarah Watts of Wellingborough, who learned to make lace forty years before at school, said that hours at the schools were longer now. A twenty-four year old lacemaker, Zillah Godfrey of Stony Stratford, gave the hours as 9 a.m. to 12 noon and 2 to 4 p.m. for beginners and from 7 a.m. for girls of 12 or 13. A certain amount of work was set and when that was finished they were free to go. The mistress set the work. Catherine Curtis, aged eleven, said she made twelve heads of broad lace a day. This, in the lace she was making, was about eight inches. Lacemakers reckoned their lace in heads rather than inches, that is by scallops on the headside of the lace; or, in 'downs', the working of one length of the parchment pattern. Another girl, aged fifteen, made twenty-four heads of narrow lace, about eighteen inches, in a day. There seems to have been a definite grading of hours according to age; four or five hours for the youngest, six or eight hours for girls; but the young women might work for twelve or fourteen hours a day to earn 3s a week. Girls of ten to thirteen might earn from 1s to 2s a week. The amount paid to the school mistress was at this time usually 3d a week.

In his report on the area Major Burns, having also heard the evidence of medical men, concluded that the lace industry, as carried on in these schools, was injurious to health, particularly to that of the younger children, who were set to work crowded together in small, ill-ventilated rooms, bending over their pillows. Consumption was a prevalent and mortal disease in the area. One doctor thought that 'much injury ensues to young girls from a habit they have of wearing a strong busk in their stays to support them when stooping over their pillows'. But the general conditions of rural life in the area, the shortages of food and fuel as income from the industry diminished, were probably an equal cause of ill health. There were few complaints of harsh discipline. According to Catherine Curtis, 'When the girls are idle missus beats them with a stick but not much to hurt them, only to make them mind her, and even then they won't mind.'[18]

According to the census of 1851 there were 5,725 children between five and fifteen years old working in the industry in the three counties, fifty-five of them boys: of these 1,754 were under ten, twenty-five of them boys.

The Lacemakers' Craft

The pillow on which the lace was worked was sometimes round, sometimes cylindrical, and stuffed tight and hard with straw. The making of lace pillows was a specialised task in the area. One maker of pillows was William Keep, Cotton End, Bedford.[19]

The pillow was supported on a 'horse' or 'maid'. These were of two types: a two-legged one with a curved bar across the top, which could not stand alone, but supported the pillow on one side while its other side rested on the knees of the lacemaker; and a three-legged one with a half hoop at the top on which the pillow rested, which stood alone. The pillow was covered with a cloth before the parchment pattern was pinned on it. The parchment had pieces of linen or cotton sewn to its ends which still remain on many surviving examples. They were known as 'eaches' and enabled a strong pull to be given to the parchment before pinning it closely to the pillow, without damaging the ends of the pattern. A second cloth was pinned over the parchment between it and the worker, to take the wear of the movement of the bobbins. This was known as the 'worker'. A third cloth, a long strip, went over the lace as it was worked to keep it clean, the 'drawter'. Finally, a cloth covered the whole pillow and its lace when it was put aside.

The linen thread was wound on to the necks of bobbins by a bobbin winder. This was a wooden wheel fixed to a stand, with a smaller wheel and holder for a bobbin at the opposite end. A band passed round the wheels and the large wheel was turned by a small handle so that the bobbin also turned and was filled with thread from a skein stretched out on four wooden arms also attached to the stand. When the bobbin was full, the thread was hitched and the bobbins were hung from a pin or pins on the pillow behind the pattern, and worked into it. The first section of the lace was worked out and the first pins stuck into the holes of the parchment to hold each twist or stitch in place. In most patterns there were possibilities of individual treatment in the texture of the clothwork and in the number and placing of the bobbins, and this was worked out by the lacemaker on the pillow. It was here that the greatest skill was needed, and this working out was called 'setting up' or 'learning a lace'. Keeping the proper length of thread released from the bobbins while working was the sign of a competent lacemaker; 'wagginwhips' was the scornful term for long, dangling bobbins which spoilt the tension on threads and so the texture of the lace.

East Midlands lace was worked with the foot, or footside, that is the straight edge which is sewn to a garment, on the worker's right. The opposite side, often worked in scallops, was known as the head or headside, and the amount of work done was reckoned by the number of scallops or heads completed. Lace was also described by the number of pins in each head, for example 'six-score' or 'four-score' lace, as the number of pins would give some measure of the intricacy of pattern and the fineness of the ground. The pins were of fine brass and it was the custom to use conspicuous bead-headed pins along the foot and head of the lace so that the worker could avoid them as she rapidly moved the pins from the back of her work to the newly twisted portion before her. To keep a firm edge to the lace it was necessary to keep these flanking pins in for a greater length than those in the middle of the work. The separate heads, with which pins were made before the middle of the nineteenth century, made it easy to replace their small brass heads with a coloured glass bead. Sometimes the burs of goosegrass were used instead, giving the plant its local name of pin-bur.

The thread was, until the nineteenth century, a fine linen thread imported from Holland. The 'gimp' (cordonnet) was a thicker, more lustrous thread, but still of linen. The lacebuyer supplied the thread to his workers for its quality was important, but to the lacemakers its cost seemed high in proportion to the amount they earned by making it up into lace. Imported linen thread paid a heavy duty, 5s a pound in 1804. In 1794 it was estimated that 3s in the £1 of the lacemakers' earnings went in thread. In 1808 another estimate was one-eighth of earnings.[20] After 1815 a fine cotton thread of British spinning was available which was suitable for lacemaking. It was cheaper and easier to use, but produced a less firm and durable lace than that made with linen thread. Working with the finest linen thread needed a developed delicacy of touch, for the bobbins had to be pulled tight, but if pulled too tight the thread snapped. Cotton was not generally used until the 1830s. Being forced to buy thread from a dealer was yet another hardship to the lacemakers in the 1840s, 'Lace does not by a third fetch near what it formerly did, they are compelled to take their thread from the dealers at the same enhanced price as formerly, and if they did not buy their thread of them they would not take their lace.'[21]

The bobbins used in the East Midlands industry during the eighteenth century were bobbins of the Flemish type, a short wooden bobbin with a shaft swelling out at the base and a single neck on which the thread was wound. In the nineteenth century this type persisted on the Continent, but in the East Midlands the shaft became longer, uniformly slim, and was weighted by a ring of beads, a 'spangle', at the bottom. A second very short neck was shaped at the top, resembling that of the French bobbins. Varied and ingenious ornament was then applied to the slender shaft. Bobbins fall into two main groups: those made of wood, mainly fruitwood; and those made of bone. Wooden ones are decorated with small inlays of different coloured wood; with pewter spots or bands; with brass wire wound closely, or in a variety of cross-garterings round the shaft, plain or threaded with tiny beads. More elaborate still were those with the shaft hollowed out into compartments with shaped openings, 'church-window'; or with a small ball or miniature bobbin within the hollow, 'mother and babe' or 'cow and calf'. Sometimes names or inscriptions were pricked on them in red and blue dots, but this was less usual for wooden bobbins than for bone ones. The decoration lavished on wooden bobbins was surpassed by that given to bobbins of bone. They, like the wooden ones, were ornamented with brass wire and brass wire threaded with beads; with gilt metal strip sunk into grooves; bound with pewter bands, or studded with pewter spots. In bone too there were church-window and mother-and-babe bobbins. But above all bone bobbins were inscribed. The inscriptions were made in small dots, picked out in red and blue, sometimes down the length of the shaft or, for longer mottos, spirally.

These inscriptions reflect the lives of the lacemakers and their times. Most common of all were those inscribed with a single name, sometimes with an added endearment, 'Dear Charles'; or with full name, sometimes with the date and name of village added, 'Ann Coulson Astcote 1840'. They record events sad or joyful in the lives of their owners, 'Rose Ann Judd died Jany 1862 aged 6 week'; and celebrate public occasions, 'May the Prince of Wales with Glory Wed'. One notable group commemorates local murderers, 'Joseph Castle Hung 1860'. Some inscriptions were religious, ranging from the simple, 'I love Jesus', to texts. They carried messages of love in all its moods, 'When this you see remember me', 'Kiss me quick my lovely dear', 'Love buy the ring', 'Tis hard to be slited by one as I love'.

The making of bobbins was another local occupation arising from the lace industry. The Haskins family were bobbin and beadmakers in Bedford in the first half of the nineteenth century. Shin bone was used for bone bobbins, which were turned on a lathe and the openwork was cut with a fine circular saw. A small drill was used for the dotted letters of the inscriptions and for the holes to fix brass-wire decoration. The spangle of a bobbin was a wire ring, threaded with seven beads, passing through a hole drilled at the bottom of the shaft. A large central bead was flanked by squarish beads of clear glass or coloured blue, red or green, which were known as 'white cuts', blue cuts', 'red cuts', and 'green cuts'. The beads were pressed on the sides with a file as they were made, and this produced both the shape and the dinted markings which can still be seen on the beads of an old spangle. The central bead was a larger, more elaborate one. Wooden bobbins were made by John Abbot of Foster Hill Road, Bedford, mainly of plum. Another maker of wooden bobbins was George Lumbis of Renhold.[22] Bobbins were sold at local markets and fairs and were often inscribed to order, the order being given on one market day and the bobbin collected on the next. It was the custom of the second Thomas Lester (Pl. 50a) to present bobbins to lacemakers for particularly good work, and examples inscribed 'A gift from Lester' survive.[23]

3 Thomas Lester and his Lace 1850-70

In spite of the industry's problems Thomas Lester was well established as a lace manufacturer by the early 1830s. The St Peter's rate books of the early 1830s show him living in Harpur Street; by 1839 he was in Tavistock Street with additional land in Offa Street and owning houses in Dame Alice Street and High Street. The following year he moved to the High Street property where he lived and where the business was carried on until his death in 1867. In 1851 the household there was Thomas Lester, his wife Elizabeth, sons Charles and Thomas and daughter Elizabeth. The elder daughter, Sarah, born in 1822, was probably already married. Two other daughters had died, Hannah at the age of twelve, and an earlier Elizabeth in infancy. From 1836 Thomas Lester had been a deacon of the Baptist Church and one of its Trustees, and was prominent in the branch chapel at Goldington and Superintendent of its Sunday school.[24]

In 1839 he was one of five lace dealers in the town; the others were Samuel Clarke, Ampthill Street; Sarah Peers, High Street; Robert Thorp, St John Street; and Martha Wilkins, Queens Head Lane. All these names had also been in the 1830 directory; two others recorded then had disappeared by 1839. Other dealers in the county were Thomas Haynes of Ampthill; Samuel Abrahams of Kempston; William Bithrey and George Paine, who were also grocers, of Turvey; Thomas Collier of Sharnbrook; and Joseph Parker of Chellington. There is little evidence to reveal the working of Thomas Lester's business and the lace it produced at this time. He issued a trade card, probably in the 1840s, showing a woman at a lace pillow, 'T Lester Lace Manufacturer. Bedford Lace Veils and Falls transferred' (Pl. 1). The word 'transfer' suggests that he employed workers who re-mounted lace on to machine-made net, as in Honiton application lace.

The veils would have included bonnet veils. During the 1830s these were large, about a yard square, usually with a patterned border on three sides and, on the fourth, a hem to take a drawstring of narrow ribbon. The veil was tied round the base of the crown to fall over the wide brim of the bonnet. As the bonnet shape changed in the 1840s these veils became smaller, and smaller still as the bonnets grew smaller in the 1850s and 1860s, when a semi-circular veil which just reached the chin became the usual form (pl. 43). A narrow frilling of lace often edged the inside of the bonnet brim in the 1840s and 1850s, so that this, rather than the hard line of the brim itself, might frame the face.

Falls could be any addition to dress of wide lace which hung freely in the way of a veil or flounce. At this time it might also mean the deep lace collar, fashionable on the low neckline of evening dress from the late 1830s until the 1860s (Pl. 44). From the 1840s these collars were often given the French name *berthe*,

14

Trade card of Thomas Lester, 1840.

or its anglicised form bertha. An alternative to this single fall of wide lace was a shaped collar of several rows of narrow lace, mounted on machine net and trimmed with ribbon bows at centre front and on the shoulders.

The Lester Collections

In 1945 Bedford Corporation received a bequest from Miss Amy Lester, daughter of the second Thomas Lester, a collection of lace, drafts, patterns, sample books and exhibition medals from her father's business. No list of the items was made until the material was deposited in the Cecil Higgins Art Gallery in 1949; BML 1- 160, 243, 377, 383. Other material which came to the Cecil Higgins Art Gallery from the Borough Library in 1950, BML 370, may also be part of this collection exhibited there before the Corporation had a museum, but again no inventory of this group of material existed prior to its cataloguing at the Art Gallery. Bedford Museum, which as Bedford Modern School Museum was in existence many years before the town had a public museum, also received items connected with the Lester business.

Before the second Thomas Lester retired in 1903 Miss Elizabeth Driver had joined him in the business which continued as Lester and Driver until 1913. It was then taken over by Miss Haines who dealt mainly in materials and equipment for needlework and knitting. When Miss Haines retired in 1952 Mr T. W. Bagshawe acquired some items still remaining in the stock taken over by Miss Haines from Lester and Driver. These are now part of the Bagshawe collection in Luton Museum.

In addition to the material preserved in the Lester family and these items which remained in the shop in the Arcade where the business moved after Thomas Lester died, material which had been dispersed was acquired by others with various interests in lacemaking. Some of this extra material has now, after passing through different hands, arrived in museum collections in Bedfordshire and elsewhere. The collection at Luton Museum contains a large number of pattern drafts, many of them given to the museum by Miss C. C. Channer in 1941, 23/41. Miss Channer had worked in the revival of point ground lace since 1897, first in Northamptonshire and then in Bedford until she retired in 1940. She was a skilled lacemaker and teacher and able to design patterns for point ground lace. During her years of work to keep the craft alive she had saved a large number of drafts from destruc-

15

tion. Many of them are inscribed with the names of dealers, including a number marked 'Lester'; sometimes they also have a date, a note of the thread to be used and another name and place name, probably showing the lacemaker and her village, or perhaps an agent in the village. Miss Channer gave drafts to others interested in the lace industry as well as to Luton Museum, and two separate groups from her collection have come through intermediaries to the Cecil Higgins Art Gallery, BML 350, 374. In these groups too some of the drafts are inscribed 'Lester', and a parchment pattern for a handkerchief border is stamped 'C and T Lester'.

The earliest item in the Lester collection is a book of lace samples, showing the type of lace Thomas Lester would have dealt in when he first set up business in Bedford, although it is doubtful whether it shows his own lace BML 1 (Pl. 2). The book, parchment bound, was originally an account book of the surveyors of the highways at Olney, forty-three pages covering the years 1783—90. The book has been re-used as an album, and small samples of lace mounted on dark blue, blue or grey card are pinned to the written pages. All the samples are point ground; most are worked with the Lille ground though a fair number have a wire ground. The possible range of date is 1800 to 1850. Although a sample book like this might have been compiled to show a manufacturer's range of patterns, it could have been a source book of possible designs, and might well have been acquired by Thomas Lester from another dealer who had ceased to trade. The Olney origin of the book suggests that it may once have belonged to one of the Olney dealers. There is a second album of samples, BML 2, within a parchment folder, formed of lengths of dark blue linen, sewn together to form pages. Small pieces of lace of the same period have been pinned on to the dark blue linen with pins of the early type, made in two parts with separate bead-like heads. A third book of samples, from the stock still in Miss Haines's shop in 1952, is in Luton Museum (Pls 3-5). This was said to have come from John Spencer, lace manufacturer of Welling-borough (flor. 1850—80). There are no names or written entries, only thirty-three folio sheets of grey paper on which small samples of lace have been stuck. From their style they appear to date from the 1820s until perhaps the end of the century. Eight sheets show laces of the type made after 1850. The widths of the lace vary from a quarter of an inch to four inches.

These sample books show a rich variety of design in the narrow borders and insertions from the earlier part of the century. They show borders with straight-edged, scalloped or vandyked edging; and the insertions which were used a great deal in dress before 1840. There are geometric patterns and patterns based on the natural forms of leaf and flower. They show the lightest of patterning, slight tendrils of clothwork outlined with a lustrous gimp which stands out as if it were a thread run through the net and the more elaborate scrolled patterns with varied fillings of the 1840s. There is also a wide range of quality. Some show East Midlands lace of the first half of the century at its best, simple and unpretentious, with formalised floral patterns and subtle geometric ones, against a fine mesh ground, finely worked (Pls 3-5). Other sheets reveal the weakening of design and workmanship and the final effect of the industry's decline on East Midlands lace.

We may be a little nearer to Thomas Lester's own work in two exercise books, BML 243. One contains drawings for lace, the first stage in preparing a pattern; the other contains drafts, the second stage, pricked on thin paper and stuck into the book; there are also similar drafts, loose. The first book contains pencil drawings on transparent paper, with the pattern shaded in pencil and the ground area left plain (Pl. 6). They have at some time been used for pricking as there are pin

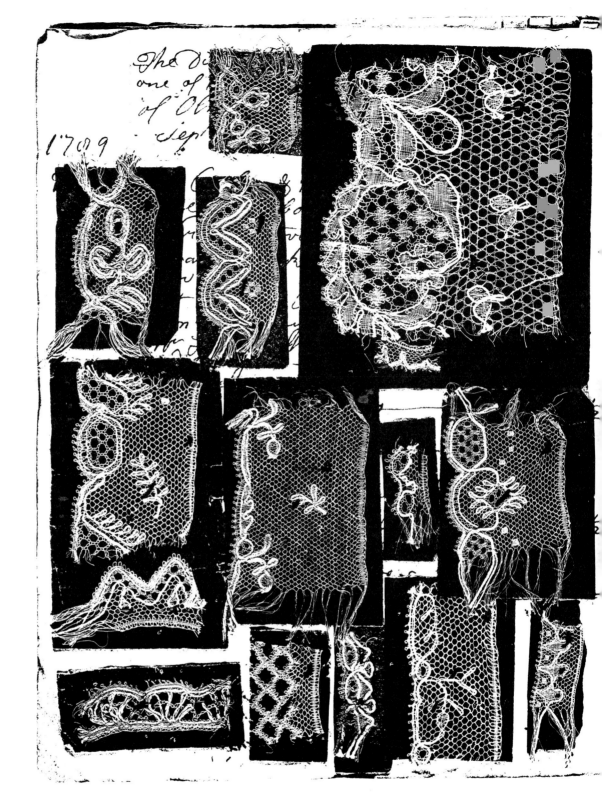

Page from album of lace
samples, 1800—50, originally
the account book of the surveyors of the highways,
Olney, Bucks., 1783—90.
Even the small selection
shown on a single page shows
a range of quality in design
and workmanship. The
widest border here has a wire
ground, in a design of
1830—50; the diminishing
clothwork characteristic of
the early nineteenth century
can be seen (centre, second
from left), and a poorer
quality lace of the same type
(bottom, second from right);
the fillings are honeycomb
stitch and two versions of
meshed clothwork.

BML 1

Actual size.

17

3 Page from album of lace samples, said to have belonged originally to John Spencer, lace manufacturer, Wellingborough, (flor.1850–80) which remained in the Lester and Driver shop in the Arcade, Bedford, until 1952. Most of the lace appears to be earlier than 1850.
Borders, 1820–40: 1 5/8 in to 3 3/8 in (4 cm to 8.6 cm) wide. The bulk of East Midlands lace at this time was in borders of these widths or a little wider, and these are characteristic patterns. Four pairs of bobbins were used to work the footside in East Midlands lace, so that four threads appear along it whereas Lille lace, worked with three pairs, shows only two threads.
Luton Museum BL1/383/55
Reduced: page size 15 3/8 in x 11 1/2 in (39 cm x 29 cm).

4 Page from same source as Pl. 3.
Insertions, 1800–50: 1/2 in to 2 3/4 in (1.3 cm to 7 cm) wide. Insertions of lace were often worked into the fabric of the white muslin dresses of 1800–30, or inserted in place of plain seams. Narrow borders and insertions of this kind continued to be used in dresses and caps for babies, and were often called 'baby lace'. The use of the gimp thread woven into the ground to make a contrasting solid band, vandyked, perhaps reflects the influence of the new fashion for embroidery on machine net, in which a similar effect is achieved by a darned thread (fifth row from bottom, extreme left; seventh row, second from left; Pl. 3 top row, extreme left).

20

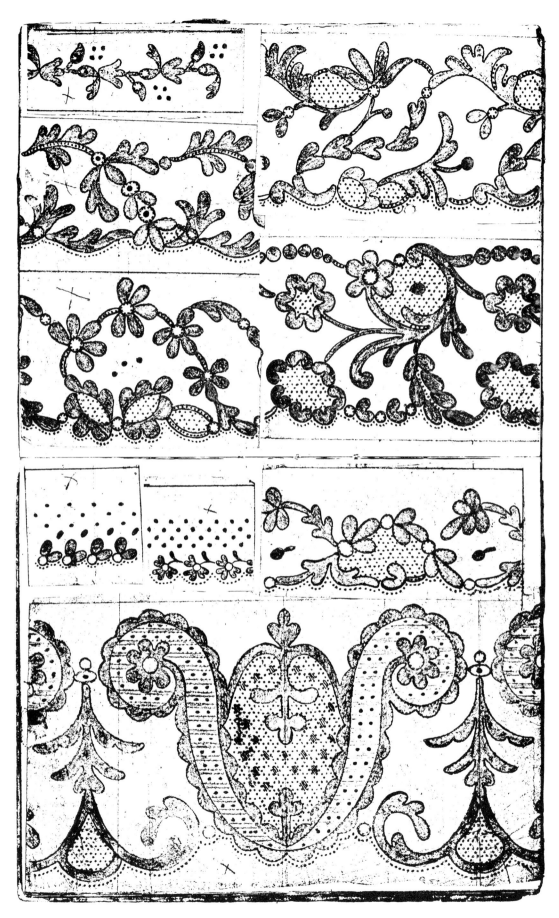

5   Part of page from the same
source as Pls 3 and 4.
Borders, 1830—50: actual size.
Heavier patterning and a
loss of the crisp contrast
between pattern and ground
notable in early nineteenth-
century work appears in the
1840s.

6   Two pages of an exercise
book of pencil drawings for
lace, 1830—50. They are
drawn on transparent paper,
the pattern shaded in and
the fillings, but not the
ground, marked. The widths
of the patterns are from
half an inch to four inches
(1.3 cm to 10 cm).

BML 243

Actual size.

21

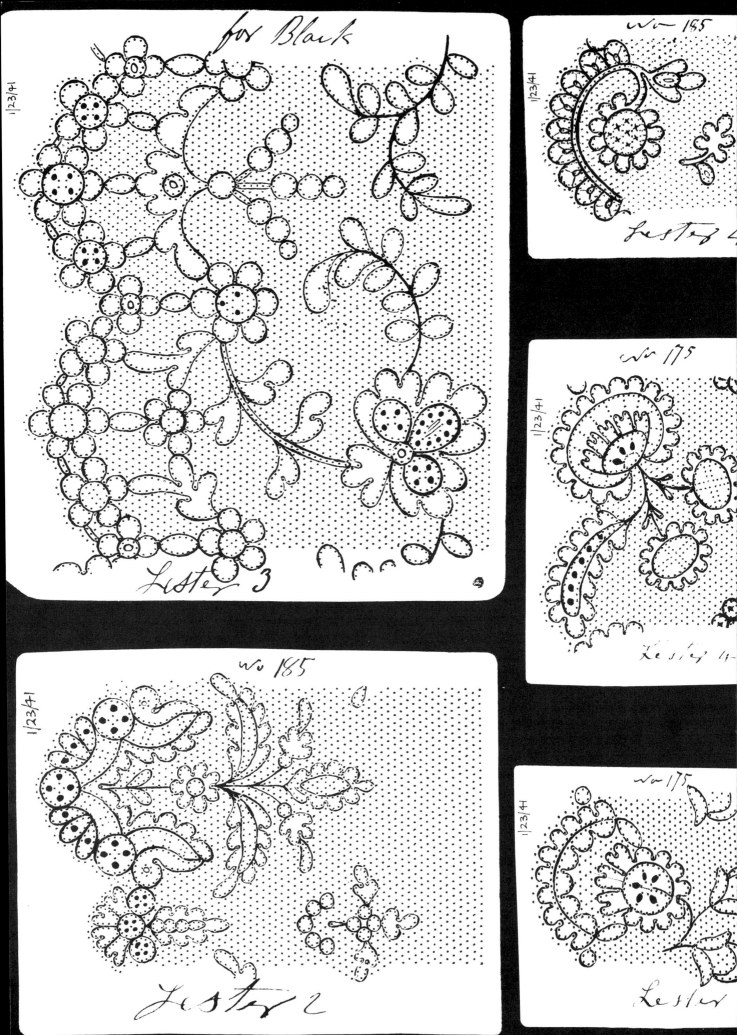

8 Drafts for point ground
lace inscribed 'Lester', 1840—
50, showing flat, flower-head
patterns which can be seen
in the laces of Pls 3 and 5, but
appear here in rather stiffer,
heavier form; and a wide
border in the 1840s style
for black lace.
Luton Museum 1/23/41
Actual size.

Drafts for lace, pricked on
thin paper or card with the
ground filled in, dated 1846.
Some of these are in an
exercise book similar to that
of Pl. 6, others loose.
Actual size.

BML 243

23

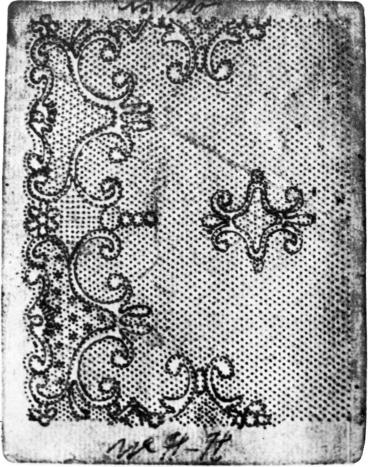

24

9 Drafts for point ground lace, inscribed 'W.H.H.', one dated 2.2.41. (W.H. Handscomb, Newport Pagnell, 1841), examples of the finer quality drafts of this time.

Luton Museum 1/23/41
Actual size.

0 Draft for handkerchief border, point ground lace, 840—60; simplified design ased on a few elements of arlier floral patterns and howing the loss of the arlier quality of this type of ace.

BML 377(5)
ctual size.

11　Draft for handkerchief
border in point ground lace,
1840–60, not completely
pricked; with notes of fillings;
design of same character as
Pl. 10.
BML 377(11)
Actual size.

26

12   Draft for handkerchief
border, rose and water lily
design, 1855—70, showing
freer, more naturalistic
drawing of flowers and a
pattern without ground. The
inner edge is marked for a
looped finish to lie over the
join with the muslin centre
of the handkerchief. See also
Pl. 23.
        BML 377(16)
Actual size.

27

13   Parchment pattern for
cap, point ground, 1840–60,
showing the end of a lappet;
compared with the handkerchief borders of Pls 10 and
11, this shows the finer
quality work still carried out
in point ground lace, in pieces
shaped for dress. This pattern, which remained in the
shop in the Arcade until
1952, is faintly stamped with
the address of Mr A. A.
Carnes, Bedford.
 Luton Museum BL5/282/55
Actual size: overall length of
pattern (half the cap) 21 in
(53 cm).

28

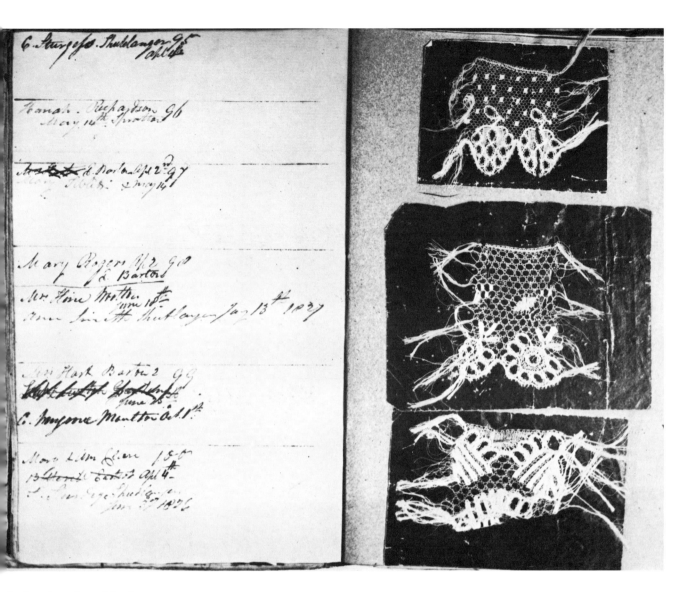

4   Lace buyer's work book
Northamptonshire, 1827,
with the names and villages
of lacemakers and the dates
of collecting as well as
samples of lace.
   Luton Museum 48/32.
Reduced: page size 7 1/4 x
4 3/4 in (18.4 x 12 cm)

15   Drafts for lace, 1855–7,   ▶
inscribed 'Lester'. These
show the new type of lace
of the 1850s without a
ground, the pattern linked
by twisted or plaited bars:
two of the drafts are marked
for the ground formed with
small plaits which give a
heavy square mesh, shown in
the draft by heavy dots;
another has the plaited
ground framed by bars, with
unusual marking at the intersections.
   Luton Museum 5/23/41
Actual size.

29

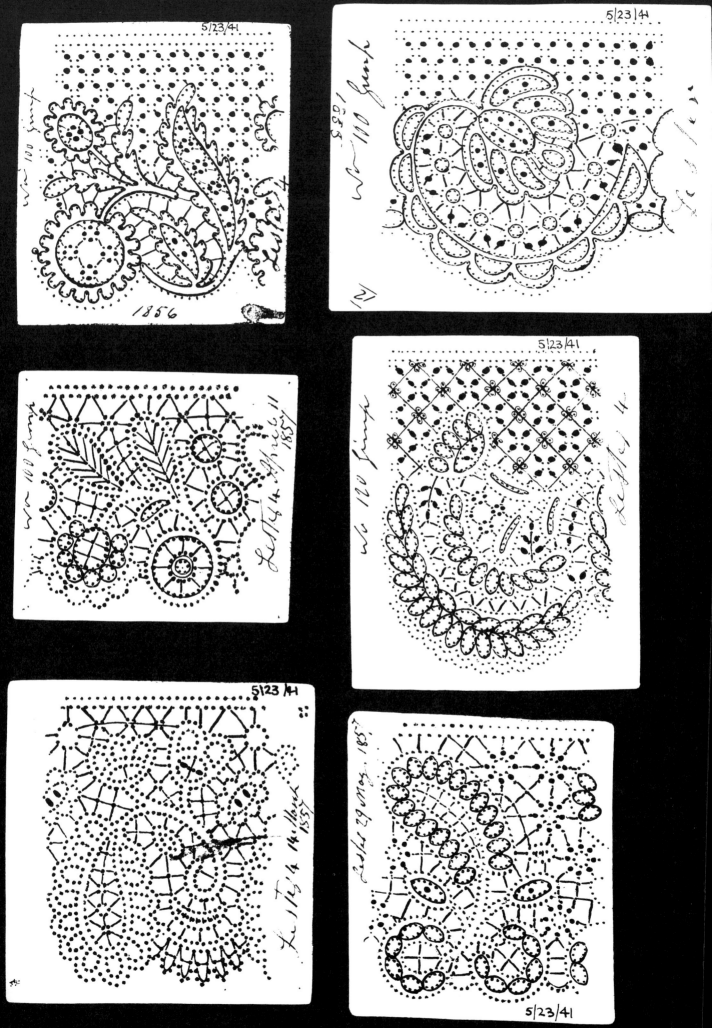

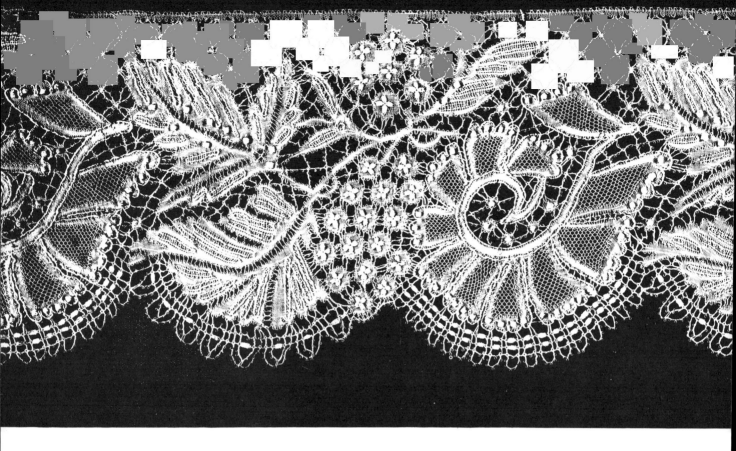

16 Drafts for lace, 1857, inscribed 'Lester'. These show the breaking up of the floral forms of Pl. 15, which have been carried over from the point ground patterns of Pl. 8 and have been given more formalised shapes, including coil and cone patterns, in this new type of lace without ground.
Luton Museum 5/23/41
Actual size.

17 Border, fruiting vine design, with trellis ground of open bars with picots, clothwork at intersections; point ground fillings; leaves veined with openwork; plaits laid in groups on clothwork. The looped edging is of two different patterns alternating in the two heads which are the unit of the design, 1860–80.
BML 4
Actual size.

18 Draft for Pl. 17, showing the double lines which indicate this particular ground, and draft for narrower border in the same basic design.
BML 4 BML 377(1)
Actual size.

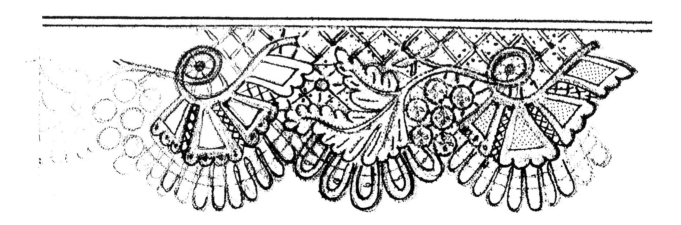

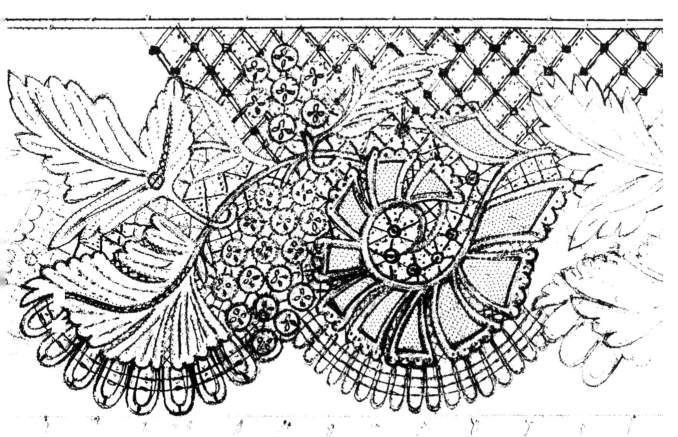

20   Flounce, convolvulus design, an elaboration of the draft
of Pl.19, with the same treatment of the headside, but
with an additional pattern of
leaves falling from the footside. The rendering of flower
and leaf shows extreme naturalism and the combination
of this with the strongly
patterned ground shows the
characteristic profusion of
mid nineteenth-century
design, 1860—80.
                        BML 9
Actual size.

19   Draft for border, convolvulus design, showing alternate
flower-head and looped
edging in the heads, the
looped edging in two different patterns, making a repeat
of three heads, 1860–80.
            BML 9(1)

Actual size.

marks round the pattern. From the style of the patterns the designs appear to have been made between 1830 and 1850 and they vary in width from half an inch to four inches. A few are initialled 'FG', 'FBG' or 'JC'. Some of the drafts in the Luton Museum collection which also have the initials 'FBG' are dated between 1847 and 1858; and some of these have another name on them together with the name of a village. The village names are Cranfield, Renhold, Wootton, Wilstead, which suggest a Bedfordshire, possibly a Bedford, source. But I have not found any one recorded as a dealer at this time with these inititals, although 'JC' could be J. Clarke of Tempsford. The drafts mounted in the second book are pricked on paper or thin card of different colours and have the ground pricked in. A few of the loose examples are dated 1846. The drafts are more stereotyped in pattern than the drawings and the outlining of the pattern area is loose and sketchy (Pl. 7).

After excluding the initialled work, there is still no evidence that these were Thomas Lester's own drawings, and his working drafts, although it is possible that both were used by him. What they do reveal is the type of lace being made at the time and something of the way the manufacturers worked, by showing first the drawing of the pattern, then the addition of the ground in the pricked draft. Miss Channer wrote of her attempts to learn how to prick a point ground mesh accurately for a new pattern as most of the point ground work at the time of the revival at the end of the nineteenth century was being worked from old patterns. Mr Smith of Olney, probably the George Smith who succeeded to John Millward's business, showed her his 'cards', which he had always used, 'pieces of white card pricked all over with holes as required for working the net ground'. He did not know who had made them nor where they had come from, 'we always had them'. The earlier dealers would have pricked out these cards for different types and sizes of mesh, as Miss Channer herself did by a method described in her book.[25] There is a pricking of ground only, on parchment, in the Luton Museum collection.

Lace in which pattern and ground are worked together, as in the East Midlands, imposes a discipline of design in the adjustment of mesh and pattern from which the lace made in two stages, as in Devon, is free. The designer needs either a working knowledge of lacemaking or the close co-operation of a lacemaker. Thomas Lester may have learnt to make lace, for there were some men as well as women who practised the craft, or he might have had the help of his wife Elizabeth who, born and brought up in Bedford, may well have been a lacemaker. At the time Thomas Lester was establishing himself as a Bedford lace manufacturer, John Roberson of Turvey, who like Thomas Lester was a Baptist, left Stevington Baptist Church £150 to build a manse, money which he had earned 'by working at the lace-pillow, denying himself of comforts and travelling to London, etc. on foot to save tolls purposely to sell his lace.'[26]

Although in the Luton Museum collection there are many drafts inscribed 'Lester' and many are dated, none has a date before 1850, and only a few are for point ground lace. One of these, a narrow border, is dated 1852; another undated has a small figure with very little clothwork within the outlining gimp. Both are earlier in character than the rest of the Lester point ground drafts, which are likely to be later than 1850 as their patterns are very close to the floral patterns in dated drafts of the 1850s without the mesh ground (Pl. 8). The point ground drafts of Lester here have not the quality of those of some of the other dealers of the 1840s, notably John Millward of Olney and W. H. Handscomb of Newport Pagnell. Some of Handscomb's drafts are in the Luton collection, including one dated 2.2.41.(Pl. 9).

Amongst the drafts, BML 377, in the Cecil Higgins Art Gallery which are undated but also likely to be after 1850 are a number for shaped pieces of lace, particularly handkerchief borders. Some are for point ground work and show both its continuing use in Lester lace and the character of point ground design at this time; one of them shows a draft in the making, with ground and fillings noted but not fully pricked (Pls 10, 11). The other is in the new style of Lester lace, a bold floral design, linked by bars (Pl. 12).

The working pattern for the lacemaker was pricked from the draft on to a strip of parchment, the unit of the design being repeated several times. In the flourishing days of the industry the pricking out of patterns may have been specialised work. In Pigot's Directory of 1839, Joseph Wooding of Harrold was described as a parchment pricker. The parchments were distributed by the dealer and towards the end of the century some, including Lester parchments, were stamped with the dealer's name. The Lester ones are stamped 'C and T Lester' which places them in the last thirty years of the century, although an earlier parchment still in use might also have been stamped in this way. By this time a stiff glazed card was being used as well as parchment. Some of the fine and obviously early point ground pieces have been stamped with the name of one of the Associations, for one of their objects was to collect and preserve the best of the early patterns. A group in Bedford Museum, including old and new point ground parchments, are stamped 'Bedford Lace Association'; amongst them is a particularly fine one for a deep flounce. Some of those in the Cecil Higgins Art Gallery are stamped A. A. Carnes, with a Bedford address and these also include fine early patterns. Mr Carnes had collected and preserved these while working for the survival of the industry and the revival of the making of point ground lace in the early years of this century, and had presented them to the town in 1924. His stamp is also on a point ground pattern for a cap in Luton Museum, which was amongst the material acquired from Miss Haines as old stock of the Lester business (Pl. 13).

Amongst the material in Luton Museum which came from Miss Channer is a lace-dealer's work book, 48/32 (Pl. 14). This is a small notebook of alternate greyish blue and white pages. On the white pages are the names of workers and their village, each with a number and date. An occasional entry of the year shows that the book was in use mainly in 1827. Sometimes there is a note '2 parchmts' against a name. On the opposite coloured pages there are samples of lace, mounted first, like those of the Olney book, on dark blue paper. Most of these appear to belong to the date of the entries, but other samples, more loosely woven in less fine thread appear to have been tacked on to the pages later and to be of later date, c. 1840. The earlier examples have a thick soft gimp round the patterns, characteristic of East Midlands lace of the 1820s, showing perhaps the influence of the contemporary fashion for blonde lace and embroidered nets. There are also some rough sketches of lace, some with a headside deeply vandyked, a shaping of dress trimmings characteristic of this decade. The names of the villages are listed each with a date, probably the date of the dealer's visit to collect lace and distribute patterns, and there is a list of the thread sold using the reference numbers of the workers. During Thomas Lester's early years in Bedford this dealer was working in villages around Northampton, within a radius of about eight miles, which suggests that he worked from the town itself. Directories list nine lace merchants there in 1823—4, five in 1830—1.

Luton Museum also received from Miss Channer three sets of manuscript instructions for working lace 125/32, 76/41; the paper on which they are written is water-marked 1818.

Thomas Lester's position as a lace manufacturer was confirmed when the lace he exhibited was awarded a prize medal at the Exhibition of the Works of Industry of all Nations, 1851, generally known as the Great Exhibition. His entry was of

'Specimens of Bedfordshire pillow lace, being an improved arrangement of an infant's lace dress; improved lace fall piece to avoid joining at corners; lace fall complete; length of wide white lace for falls; length of white and black trimming lace; length of flouncing lace.'

The 'improved lace fall piece to avoid joining at the corners' may have been lace slightly shaped to fit a low, v-shaped neckline.

The report of the jury on the lace in the Exhibition referred to the falling demand for East Midlands lace, but noted an increased demand for black silk lace, which had become fashionable during the 1830s and was to remain fashionable throughout the 1850s and 1860s. Black lace was used in effective contrast with pale or bright silks in evening wear, in flounces decorating the widening skirts and in deep collars falling from the low neckline of the bodices.

It was also effective in the square or triangular shawls of lace which, in summer wear, spread over the ever-widening expanse of the fashionable skirt, making a tracery of black on the coloured silk. When deeper, stronger colours were added to the range of colour in the late 1850s the contrast of black with a single rich colour was maintained and often brought into the silks themselves, with elaborate patterns woven in black. Narrow black laces were also used in trimmings; in the 1860s often in appliqué, that is mounted first against white silk before being added to the coloured fabric of the dress. A trimming of black lace shaped as a yoke, on the bodices of high-necked day dresses, was characteristic of the late 1860s.

Thomas Lester's main production of lace now ranged from the narrow borders to these wider laces. The award was given for his wide white and black laces. But his entry included pieces with a hint of innovation and an awareness of technical problems and, even if these were pieces made specially for exhibition purposes rather than for general sale, they suggest that he had, or could draw on, considerable skills.

Another exhibitor from Bedford, C. J. Sim, who had recently established himself in the High Street, received an honourable mention for two pairs of lappets in imitation of Mechlin lace, and various trimming laces. Other exhibitors from the East Midlands who were awarded medals were William Ayres of Newport Pagnell and R. Viccars of Padbury for wide thread lace of good quality. There were also entries from S. Vincent of Turvey, C. and T. Cardwell of Northampton and B. Hill of Olney; Elizabeth Rose of Paulerspury showed a black lace dress which she had designed and made and Elizabeth Frewen of Marlow, work of her own design, collar, cuffs, lappets and necktie.[27]

Lappets of lace had been worn in evening headdress since the eighteenth century and were still used in dressing the head for evening in the 1840s and 1850s. They were made either in pairs with one end of each rounded or in a single piece, as they are in the Lester collection. They could be worn as streamers falling from the cap or headdress or looped up with flowers and ribbon. The lace of lappets was worked without a foot. Those in the Lester collection are of even width, about 3 inches. There are narrow pieces, less than 2 inches wide and a little shorter than most of the lappets, which widen out at each end. These could have been used as lappets but were probably intended to be worn as ties, the ends crossed in front and secured by a brooch at the high neck line of the day dresses of the 1860s.

Many of the lace entries were shown by retailers not manufacturers. The number of shops in London dealing only in lace was by now greatly reduced, but several of the new departmental stores had lace departments. The two main lace retailers, of foreign as well as English lace, were Copestake, Moore, Crampton & Co. and Daniel Biddle. Amongst the lace shown by Copestake & Co. was some made at Olney from a pattern by John Millward.[28] The report on design in this class concludes, rather ambiguously,

'The greater excellence of French and Belgian lace seems to consist more in the truer appreciation of beauty of line and delicacy of form than in any very marked supremacy of design.' [29]

The Great Exhibition appears to have had a great influence on East Midlands lace and on Thomas Lester in particular. Hand-made lace of many different types from many countries had been shown there as well as a great deal of machine-made lace. From the 1850s the drafts of East Midlands manufacturers show lace of quite a different type from that previously made in the area. This new lace, given the name Bedfordshire Maltese, implied a debt to the lace of Malta which had been shown in the Exhibition, although the Jury's comment on this had been, 'Little worthy of notice from Malta'. Basically it was a return to the laces of the sixteenth and early seventeenth century with geometric patterns in plaited bars, a type of bobbin lace made in Genoa which had spread to Malta. Lace of this kind, easier to design and quicker to make than the grounded laces, seemed an answer to machine competition; and for the next few years it was.

At the London International Exhibition of 1862, T. Lester and Son, Bedford, exhibited 'Maltese pillow laces of various kinds' and received a medal 'for a variety of useful goods of good design and manufacture'. The Jury's report on class XXIV, English pillow lace, comments,

'At the Exhibition of 1851 no pillow lace was shown more than eight inches wide and the great progress made since that time may be readily perceived by an examination of the fine specimens of piece goods, including shawls, tunics, flouncing, veils, etc. which are exhibited this year and which for beauty of design and excellence of workmanship may be said not unjustly to rival those of France and Belgium. The credit for this great improvement is due mainly to the intelligent and painstaking perseverance of Mr Edward Godfroy — a native of France — who has been engaged with the English lace trade for some years and has instructed the English workers in the art of "fine-joining".'

Edward Godfroy worked from Buckingham. One of his flounces was shown in the 1862 exhibition by Debenham and Freebody, a tunic flounce of black silk lace, 38 inches deep. This continued the point ground tradition and in design and quality was very close to the lace of Chantilly, where the bobbin lace industry was maintaining its position by concentrating on fine and costly lace for a highly fashionable international market. The 'fine-joining' technique Mr Godfroy had introduced was that used by the Chantilly workers for the large pieces of lace, shawls and mantles of black silk lace. The lace was made in sections by a number of workers and then invisibly joined by a stitch known as *point raccroc*. The flounce was called a tunic flounce because lace of this width would completely cover the skirt of the dress in a single deep fall.

Apart from the reference to this work there was no special mention of East Midlands lace in the report. Once again a good deal of the lace, like this flounce, was exhibited by retailers, Hayward & Co., who had succeeded Daniel Biddle, and Copestake, Moore and Crampton. Debenham and Freebody and Howell and James were amongst the stores exhibiting, and Honiton flounces shown by them were illustrated in the *Art Journal Catalogue* of the Exhibition. A Honiton lace dress shown by Howell and James attracted a great deal of notice. From the East Midlands, Cardwell of Northampton and Viccars of Padbury who had shown at the 1851 Exhibition were again exhibiting as well as Thomas Lester. There was a new name from Bedford, J. Hornsey, who had been there since at least 1850, and was exhibiting 'Maltese and other laces and lace goods'. J. Sargeant from Sandy and Thomas Gilbert of High Wycombe exhibited 'lace articles' and 'lace goods' respectively. Much Nottingham lace and French machine lace was also shown and admired.

Amongst lace articles and lace goods were such pieces as fan leaves and parasol covers. Fans had never gone out of use but they became more fashionable from the 1860s than they had been for a generation. Amongst the fashionable fans of this time were fans of lace and these continued to be fashionable to the end of the century and beyond, although the size of the fan changed. The fan shape dictated the design of the lace and many surviving fans show some of the most attractive examples of lace design of their time, in many different types of lace. There are no examples of fan leaves in the lace of the Lester collection nor amongst the drafts and patterns. There is, however, a parasol cover. Small parasols were fashionable from the 1840s to the early 1870s and then became larger. Lace designed for a particular shape also appeared here. The lace was either a repeating design for the triangular space between two ribs or was worked out concentrically. There is one parasol cover in the Lester collection, BML 38, of coarse white lace of heavy design, probably of the 1870s or 1880s.

Most of the lace showed an increased naturalism in its designs. Honiton lace sometimes reflected the French style in which this naturalism was contained within a framework of scrolls and strapwork, but was often and characteristically worked with an almost botanical exactness in its floral pattern. The report on English pillow lace concluded by stressing once again that what the industry needed was 'not artists who can draw exquisite designs on paper, but experienced draughtsmen who link a practical acquaintance with lacemaking to their artistic capabilities.' [30]

The Lester Lace

The work of Thomas Lester and his sons during the second half of the nineteenth century can be seen in the lace of the Lester collection at the Cecil Higgins Art Gallery and in the large collection of drafts at Luton Museum where it appears in context, amongst the drafts from many other manufacturers of this time. These drafts include some signed 'Lester' and dated mainly in the 1850s, together with a large number of signed but undated ones which are very similar in design. There is no doubt that during the 1850s Thomas Lester was working vigorously on new types of lace pattern, grafting the familiar patterns of point ground into the framework which revived the working of earlier bobbin laces (Pls 15, 16).

The drafts show three different developments; geometric patterns, very close to those early laces of the late sixteenth and early seventeenth century; the introduction into these of formalised leaf and flower shapes, including the cone shape which, having developed in Indian shawls, flourished in all shawls derived from them and became an ubiquitous feature of nineteenth century textile ornament; and patterns which have a uniform ground, not the light twisted mesh of point

41

ground lace but a bolder trellis work, formed of 'plaits' or 'tallies'. These plaits which in point ground were scattered over the ground or introduced into the fillings form the sides of a new type of mesh, shown in the drafts by heavy dots. Leaf-shaped plaits, often called 'wheat ears', which are often used as fillings and are a characteristic feature of Maltese lace, are shown by small ovals. The bars or legs (Pl. 16) of the other drafts are marked by straight lines, single or double, for twists or plaits; dots pricked close to the lines show picots. The flowing clothwork trail found in many laces is pricked in continuous parallel lines. Occasionally the traditional outlining with a gimp thread still appears, shown by a line drawn round the pattern.

Although the abandoning of a point ground background to the pattern of the lace is characteristic not only of the Lester lace but of much of East Midlands lace from the 1850s onwards, point ground lace did not at once disappear. Lester himself continued to produce the traditional lace for some years and occasionally later, as the point ground draft dated 1852 in the Luton Museum collection shows. With one or two possible exceptions, it is likely that the undated drafts of point ground lace which are inscribed 'Lester' are also from the 1850s (Pl. 8). They show a floral pattern of flat and open flower heads which is heavier and more static than the sprigs of the earlier point ground patterns.

Nor was Thomas Lester the only manufacturer to use the new patterns. Another draft in the Luton Museum collection marked 'Clarke' and dated 1853, with a geometric pattern worked in deep scallops from a point ground background, shows the transition from the traditional East Midlands lace to the new form. It is difficult now to discover how far Thomas Lester was an innovator of new patterns and techniques. All the East Midlands manufacturers were working under pressure to produce hand-made laces more cheaply and all might have found new possibilities in what they had seen of other laces at the Exhibition. The Exhibition itself had created so much public interest that there was an incipient demand for products inspired by it. Names of other manufacturers and dates in the 1850s appear on many drafts, drafts very similar in pattern to those inscribed 'Lester', including some with plaited ground. Amongst them are a number with the name 'G. Abraham, Kempston' or 'Geo. Abraham Designer' stamped or written on them. One of these is dated 'Geo. Abraham, Designer, 1854'. Some have the name of a manufacturer as well as the name Abraham, including Clarke (Bedford or Tempsford) and Sargeant (Sandy); on one the name Lester has been crossed out and 'Clark' written instead. There was a lace dealer, S. Abrahams, at Kempston from 1839 to 1864. It is possible that George Abraham did actually work as a designer only; that Thomas Lester bought some designs from him, and that the drafts marked 'Lester' may show the designer identifying his customer, not Thomas Lester marking his own drafts. The hand which wrote 'Lester' and the hand which wrote 'Sargeant' could be the same. Yet George Abraham is not recorded in directories as a designer and his name and place in the industry as a designer of lace in Bedfordshire is lost except for the evidence of the drafts.

This does not mean that Thomas Lester did not also design lace himself. The Lester collection at the Cecil Higgins Art Gallery contains examples of lace similar to the lace of these drafts, but it also includes lace of a different character, deep flounces, caps and handkerchief borders of elaborate naturalistic patterns. Except for two collars made for the Chicago Exhibition which were given by Miss Lester to Mrs Terry, and to the Museum by Mrs Terry's daughter in 1962, none of the lace has any external evidence of date, although one of the collars in the main collection is similar in pattern to one of those sent to Chicago. Thomas Lester exhibited at the 1851 Exhibition, Thomas Lester and Sons at the International Exhibitions, London, 1862, Paris 1867 and C. and T. Lester at Vienna, 1873 and London, 1874. Their lace was awarded medals at all these exhibitions and the medals are preserved in the collection. It is most likely that the pieces of most elaborate design and fine workmanship were made for exhibition purposes.

Some of the pieces survive with their drafts, drawn and pricked for working on grey card. There are no parchment patterns; it is possible that these were destroyed once the lace had been exhibited or that a single working of it was made direct from the drafts. The pieces with drafts include two handkerchief borders, BML 26, 28, (Pls 21, 24); the rest are for borders of different widths. One in a fruiting vine design has lace, BML 4, and draft, BML 377 (1), of the same width (3¾ inches) (Pls 17, 18). The deep flounce, BML 9, (Pl. 20) in convolvulus design has no matching draft; although there is a draft only, BML 9 (1), for a similar design in a lesser width (Pl. 19). Flounces of the same pattern scaled to their position, deep flounces on the skirt, narrower borders for the smaller area of the bodice, were a fashionable trimming for dresses from 1840 to 1870, in printed and woven flounces as well as lace.

The deep flounce of convolvulus design is an outstanding piece of work (Pl. 20). It is a hybrid lace in its mingling of geometric and natural forms. The dominant pattern shows a natural treatment of the flowers and leaves of the convolvulus and forget-me-not, with the clothwork veined to show the structure of leaf and flower. There is a narrow band of uniform ground of complicated structure, based on the stitches of early cutwork, and this is partly veiled by a pattern of leaves falling from the foot. The head is deeply scalloped, with a repeat of three designs, one edged with flat, open flower-heads, the second and third with different treatments of a looped edging show the influence of seventeenth century lace.

The border, BML 4 (Pl. 17), is simpler, a design of grapes and vine leaves with a short repeat, a formalised coil of leaf worked in bordered half-stitch alternating with a naturalistic spray of vine leaves, worked in veined clothwork, and grapes which are small plaits laid on clothwork. The ground is a light trellis of open bars. A vine pattern is used again on a cap, BML 60, with a different ground, plaited bars with picots.

The convolvulus of the flounce appears again on one of the handkerchief borders, combined with fern leaves, BML 26 (Pls 21-23). The pattern is linked by bars with picots scattered with webs and small plaits. A forget-me-not spray is worked against an oval of point ground, which is surrounded by small plaits arranged as leaves on half stitch, to form a medallion for the centre of each side.

The other handkerchief border with its draft, BML 28 (Pls 24-26), is a rose and thistle design, a pattern repeated in other lace in the collection, two borders of different widths, BML 5, 53 (Pls 27, 28). The pattern is linked by bars with picots which have alternate webs and clothwork flowers at intersections in one row at the foot. Rose and water lily appear in a cap, BML 59 (Pls 29, 30). A cornucopia appears in several pieces, cuffs, BML 80, 88, and collar, BML 110 (Pl. 31).

One group, which includes caps, and cap lappets, BML 4, 42, 50, 54, collar and matching cuffs, BML 29, 126, and a square mat, BML 20, have a bird or animal in the design, naturalistically portrayed. The cuffs and collar show eagles (Pl. 32); the mat a stag. An ostrich appears at each end of the cap lappets, and at the ends and in the head piece of the cap, BML 54, 42 (Pls 33-35). Another cap, BML 41, has figures of macaws, and cap lappets, BML 50, giraffes. A secondary pattern of stems and leaves appears in all these pieces; each has a different ground. Naturalism in lace could scarcely be carried further than it has been here.

The handkerchief border of convolvulus and fern design is similar to a Honiton border, designed by Lady Trevelyan, worked by Miss Sansom and acquired by the Victoria and Albert Museum for £16 16s in 1864 (Pl. 36). In this the pattern is based entirely on fern leaves from several different types of fern, but it is clear that both are drawing on a common inspiration in design. The fern leaf appears again in the flounce of Honiton lace shown by Debenham and Freebody at the 1862 exhibition.[31] It was a favourite design in textiles, pottery and glass in the 1850s and 1860s (Pl. 37). In 1867 *The Queen,* reviewing the lace at the Paris Exhibition, said 'It is remarkable that in pillow and machine lace as well as in glass and engraving, many of the most beautiful designs in the exhibition are composed of ferns.' Although in the two handkerchief borders the difference between the two techniques of lacemaking has influenced the working of the design, the East Midlands work has drawn closer to Honiton lace in its texture. This greater likeness to Honiton lace can be seen in other pieces in the collection, in the cap, BML 59 (Pls 29, 30), collar and cuffs, BML 85, 146, 147. Fern leaves also appear in a cap, BML 43 (Pls 38, 39), again combined with convolvulus, but in lace very different in character from the handkerchief border.

Honiton lace had been able to adapt more easily to the changing taste of the 1840s than the lace of the East Midlands. It was more fashionable, especially after Queen Victoria had chosen it for her wedding dress, and therefore high quality lace was again made. Honiton lace shown at the 1851 Exhibition was much admired, although there was still the reservation that however good the workmanship, there was need for improvement in design. 'The patterns of Honiton lace are generally too heavy, the form rather too large and overcrowded, and the whole effect a little too solid and equal, although this partly arises from the mode of manufacture.'[32]

If Thomas Lester was not already familiar with Honiton lace, he would have seen its achievements at the Exhibition, and would have been aware that this lace had a fashionable status which his own had not. He appears to have been as much influenced by this lace as by any other at the exhibition; this influence is evident in the lace of the Lester collection and acknowledged by Thomas Lester.

When he gave evidence to the Children's Employment Commission of 1862 on the lace industry, he described the laces of the East Midlands. 'The Buckinghamshire lace is principally black and probably the greatest in value of the three; the Bedfordshire white fancy lace, in imitation of Honiton; and Northamptonshire, white thread lace of a coarser sort.'[33] When Charles Knight wrote about the industries of the South Midlands in his *Companion to the British Almanack, 1861,* he quoted a 'Bedford lace merchant' who told him that Bedford and its neighbourhood were now making lace rivalling Honiton, 'in making lace after the peculiar fashion for which the West had long been distinguished'.

Although Thomas Lester himself spoke of imitating Honiton lace, the work he produced shows a wider exploration of the techniques of bobbin lace, different combinations of lace stitches to achieve new effects in pattern and ground. This technical invention and skill produced the characteristic work of the major pieces of the collection. The two handkerchief borders, one from Bedfordshire and one from Honiton, are similar in design but show characteristic differences of working (Pls 21-23, 36). In the Honiton work leaves and flowers have a raised outlining and the open work of the veining also has a raised edge; there is no raised effect in the Lester border, only delicate veining of leaves and flowers. The Bedfordshire border is finished by a very fine edging of scalloped loops with picots, repeated where the lace joins the muslin centre, so that it lies on the muslin ground. This

44

3 Handkerchief with border in convolvulus and fern design, showing the way the [lo]oped inner edge of the bor[d]er lies over the handkerchief, [c]oncealing the join. Handker[c]hiefs like this with a deep [b]order of lace round a small area of muslin were for display not for use. They were dress handkerchiefs carried in the hand instead of a fan. 1860—80.

BML 26
Reduced: actual size 17 1/4 in. square (43 cm)

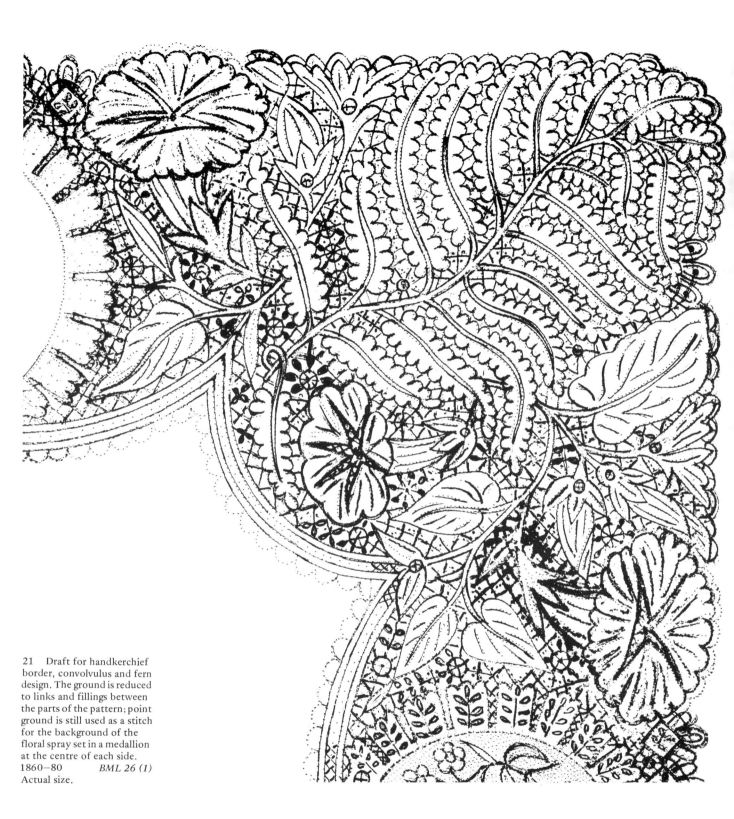

21 Draft for handkerchief
border, convolvulus and fern
design. The ground is reduced
to links and fillings between
the parts of the pattern; point
ground is still used as a stitch
for the background of the
floral spray set in a medallion
at the centre of each side.
1860–80   *BML 26 (1)*
Actual size.

Corner of handkerchief
[bor]der, convolvulus and fern
[des]ign showing the different
[trea]tment of the leaves of
[the] two plants. The indented
[fern] leaves have been care-
[full]y observed and natural-
[ism] achieved by their edges

of small scallops, each with
its own edging of a row of
small holes enclosed within
the gimp outlining thread
which is not used to outline
the other leaves, 1860–80.
BML 26
Actual size.

47

25 Corner of handkerchief ►
border, rose and thistle design.
The draft has not been
followed exactly, some of
the small flower heads and
leaves of plaits being omit-
ted and some web stitches
replaced with a plait on clothwork, 1860—80.
BML 28
Actual size.

24 Draft for handkerchief
border, rose and thistle design.
In each group of flower heads
only one is marked with the
filling stitches. There are two
types of ground, picot bars
and an elaboration of these
with web stitch; plaits on
clothwork and small flower
heads and leaves are also
scattered over the ground,
1860—80.
BML 28
Actual size.

49

26 Handkerchief with border
in rose and thistle design, two
different treatments of
centre, matching on opposite
sides, the flow of the design
maintained in one, but
broken in the other,
1860—80.

BML 28
Reduced: 14.1/2 in (36.8 cm)
square.

50

Border, rose and thistle
design, a variant of the pattern used for the handkerchief border, Pl. 26, with a
uniform ground similar to
that used in the border and
flounce, BML 9 (Pls 19, 20),
pp 60—80.

BML 53

Actual size.

Border, rose and thistle
design, variant of pattern
used in border BML 53
(Pl. 27), but simplified for
the narrower width.

BML 5

Actual size.

51

29　Headpiece of cap, rose
and water lily design. The rose
and water lily of the draft for
a handkerchief border,
BML 377 (16) (Pl. 12), appears again, in an open uniform ground of picot bars
with either clothwork or
clothwork and plait at intersections, 1860—80.

BML 59

Actual size.

30 Cap, rose and water lily design (Pl. 29). This type of cap with lappets and cap shaped together in a single flat piece rested on top of the head, on the large chignon of hair which was a hairdressing style of the late 1860s and early 1870s. There are other caps in the collection also made in a single flat piece and worn in the same way, but shaped differently, with a point to be worn in front, the lappets continuing from this to hang close together at the back of the head, BML 41, 58, 60, 1860–80

BML 59

31 Collar and cuffs, cornu- ▶ copia design; not a matching set but showing the use of this figure in slightly different patterns. The collar also shows a blurring of outline and a loss of crispness in working compared with the cuffs, 1860–90.

BML 110, 80, 88
Actual size.

54

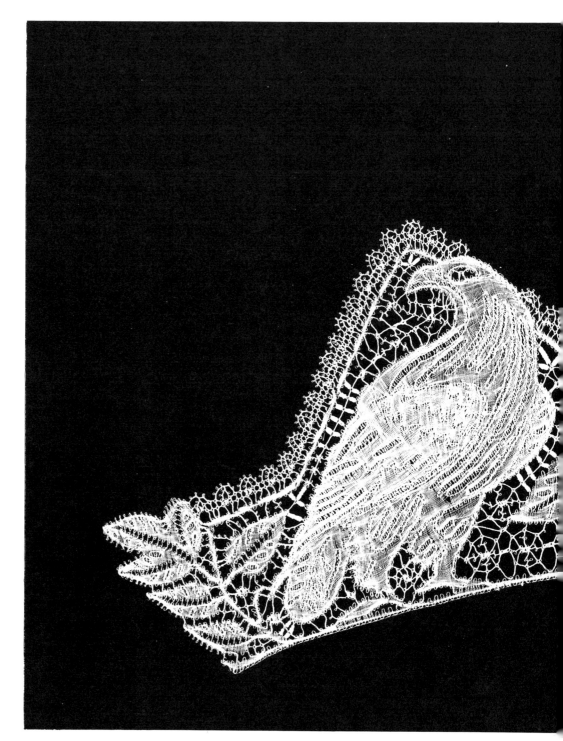

32   Cuffs, eagle design. There
is also a collar of matching pattern, shaped to enclose four
eagles, two at the back and
one at each front end. The
naturalistic treatment of the
bird dominates the design,
but the cuffs also show an
excellent example of a
looped edging, 1860–80.
                    BML 126
Actual size.

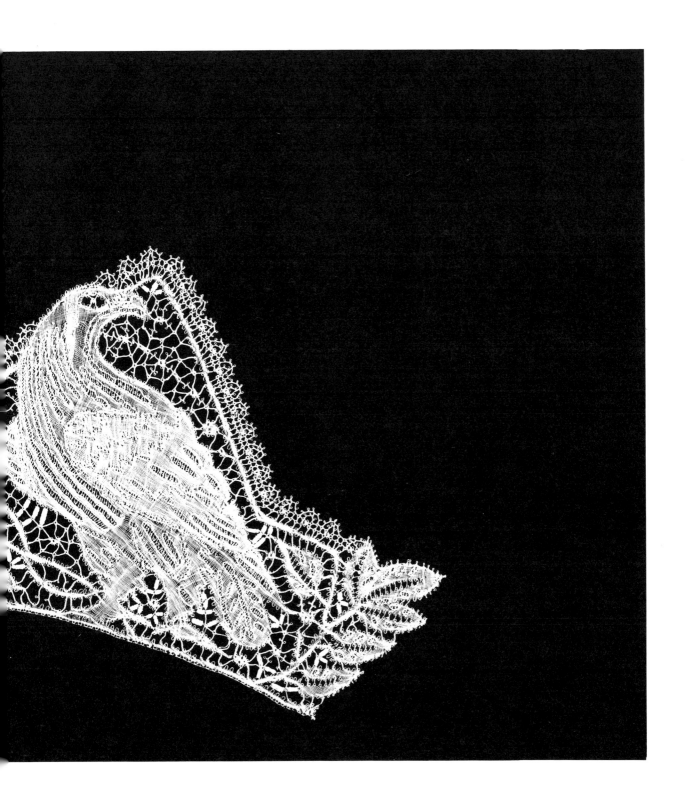

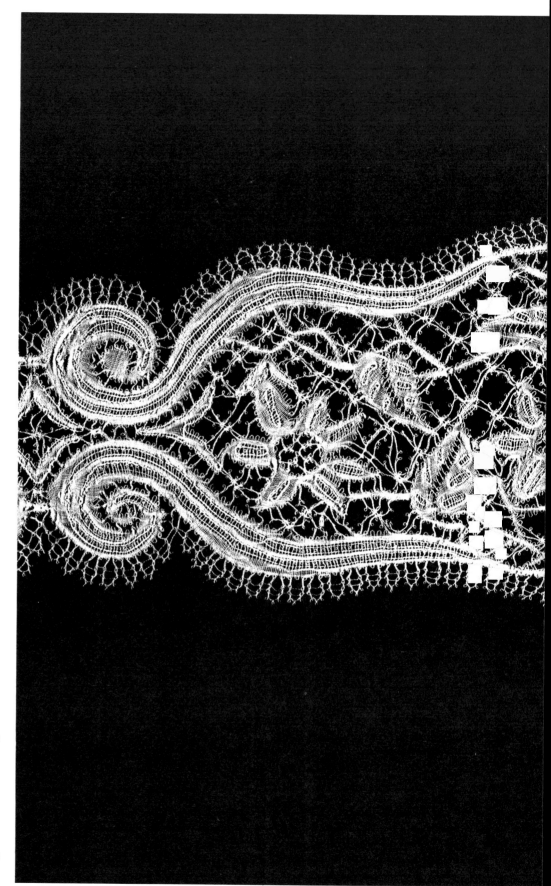

33   Cap lappets, ostrich design.
These are made in a single piece
with the figure of the bird at each
end. They could be worn, as in
the 1850s, without a cap, over the
head, the ends loose or looped up
with ribbon and flowers: or they
could be part of a cap or headdress and again loose or looped
up with other trimming. The
ground is the same as that of the
border, BML 4 (Pl. 17) and there
is a finely worked looped edging,
1860—80.
                            BML 54
Actual size: overall length 44 in.
110 cm.

58

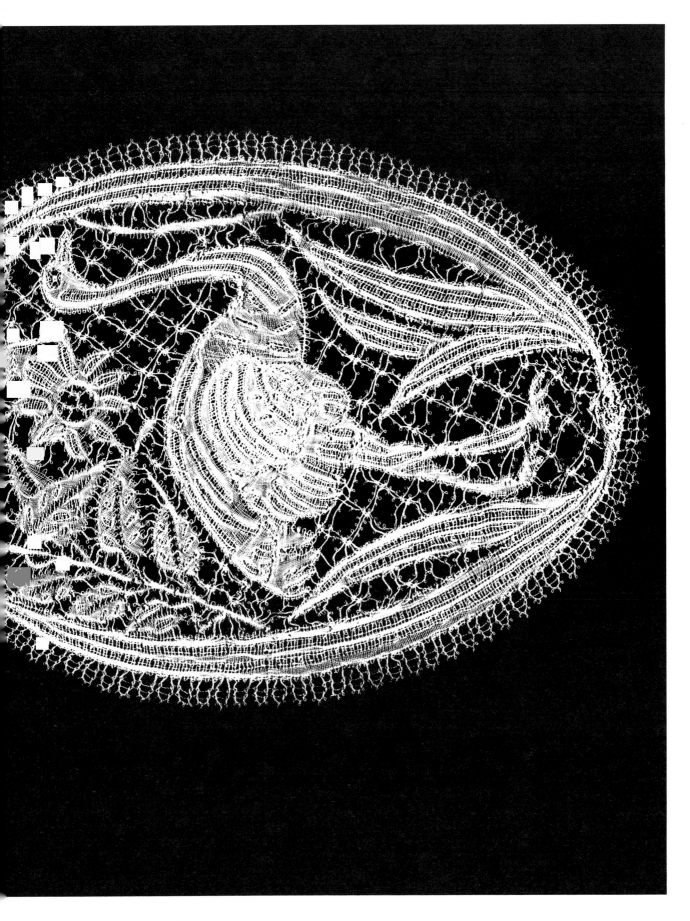

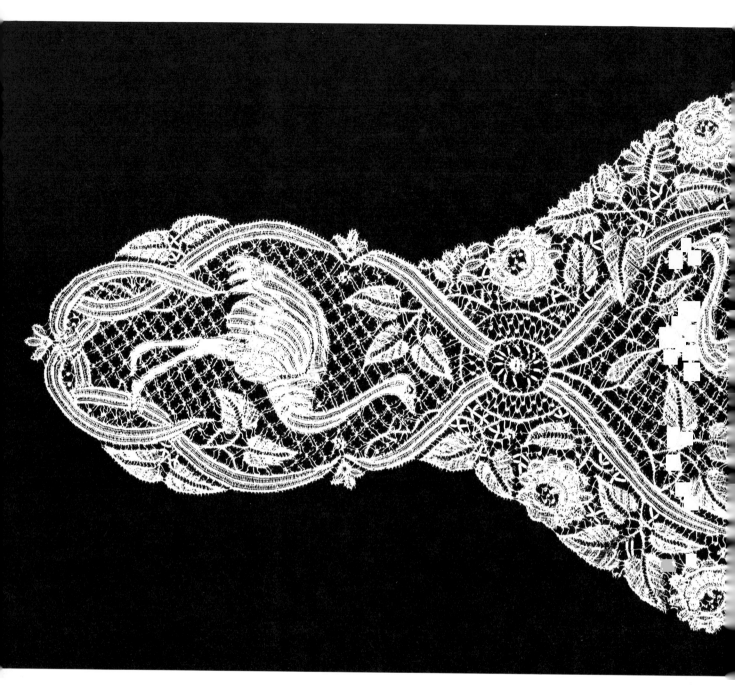

34 Headpiece of cap, ostrich
design more elaborate than
that of the lappets, BML 54
(Pl. 33). The border of rose
and thistle head encloses the
headpiece only. The ground
is the same as that of the
lappets, BML 54 (Pl. 33),
1860–80.

BML 42

Actual size.

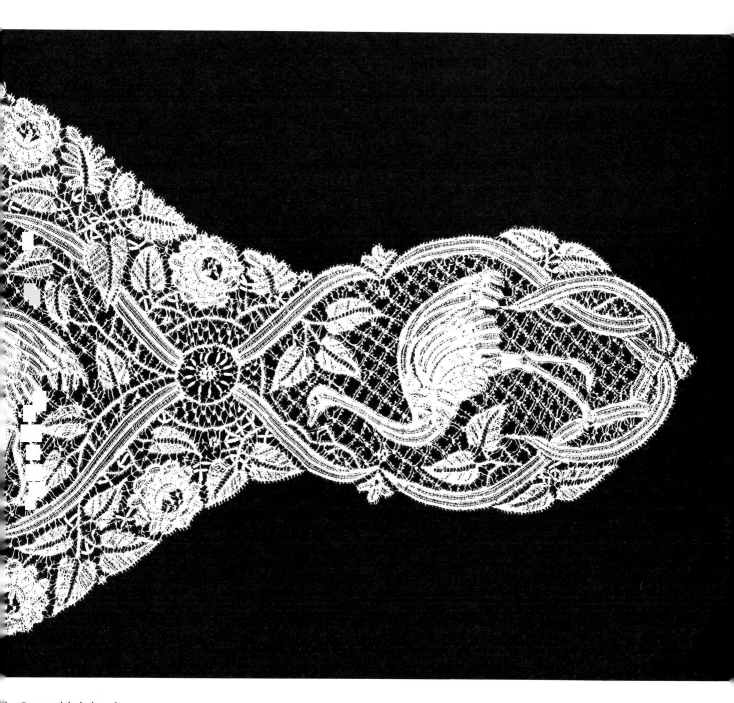

Cap, ostrich design, show-
g the linking of the three
ctions of the cap within
e extended, leaf-like
rder, similar to BML 54
l. 33): worn as BML 59
l. 30), 1860–80.
                    BML 42
educed: overall length
1/2 in (72 cm).

36   Handkerchief with
Honiton lace border in fern
design, showing naturalism in
design common to both the
new East Midlands patterns
and Devon lace at this time,
and a likeness in pattern

though the two laces are still
different in technique,
1862—4.

Victoria and Albert Museum
785, 1864
Reduced: 18 in (46 cm)
square.

7 Brocaded silk, designed
and woven at the Spitalfields
School of Design for the
Great Exhibition, 1851;
showing fern leaves amongst
the naturalistic flowers and
leaves of the design. Such
designs in other textiles at
the Exhibition may have
inspired Thomas Lester's
work in lace.
Victoria and Albert Museum
reduced.

38   Cap, convolvulus and
fern design worked in heavy
thread; a hybrid lace with
the flower and leaf worked
into a scrolled leaf pattern
similar to BML 54 (Pl. 33).
The patterned ground or
fillings and the looped
edgings emphasise the geometric character, making the
lace closer to the
Bedfordshire Maltese type in
spite of the convolvulus and
fern elements in the pattern,
1860–80.
                    BML 43
Reduced: overall length
26 1/2 in (66 cm).

66

39 Cap, convolvulus and fern
design (Pl. 38) as worn, 1860—80
BML 43

fine finish at the edge of the lace is characteristic of Lester's work, although it is not invariably used. Other examples can be seen in the vine border (Pl. 17) the flounce (Pl. 20) the lappets (Pl. 33) and several borders BML 5, 51, 53, 66, 68 (Pls 27, 28, 40, 48). Obviously derived from seventeenth century laces, it is basically a plaited loop or loops, with or without picots, treated in different ways, sometimes with small plaits added to it. The quality and finish this edging adds to a simple, narrow lace can be seen in BML 66 (Pl. 48). Such edgings, well worked, often redeem the most common Bedfordshire Maltese patterns.

The veining of petals and leaves appears in several borders as well as in the more elaborate designs. The alternate rose and thistle of a 3 inch wide border, BML 5 (Pl. 28), and the single repeating flower of BML 51 both show this technique. The thistle heads of BML 5 also show another characteristic feature, the working of plaits on clothwork to give a slightly embossed texture, used also for the grapes of the vine pattern (Pl. 17) as part of a geometric pattern in the cuffs, BML 115, and at intersections in some of the grounds. Raised lace, in which part of the pattern is lifted separately from the ground, appears in two borders of different widths, BML 68 (Pl. 40). A single, drooping flower head which forms the repeat of the pattern shows its upper petals as if concealed by bracts, which are worked in veined and outlined clothwork; these fall over the lower petals, seen from the inside and worked in plain clothwork; the centre of the flower is in Lille mesh. Here the gimp thread traditional to the East Midlands is used to outline this part of the pattern. In many of the new laces this outlining thread has been abandoned, but not entirely.

Instead of a gimp thread outlining the pattern it is often worked down the centre of a narrow clothwork trail. A corded trail appears in the traditional laces of Eastern Europe. The trail itself was characteristic of Italian bobbin laces from the Milan area and was the basis of many of the East Midlands laces in the second half of the nineteenth century. It was worked in flowing curves which often intersect to enclose formalised flower or leaf shapes, or geometric figures in clothwork or in plaits; or shaped into loops as in BML 15 (Pl. 41). The working of a gimp thread down the centre of the trail has the effect of strengthening and tightening the design and gives an added quality to lace of this type.

In these new types of lace the elements of the pattern are linked by plaited bars, with or without picots. The designers and workers now used the Lille mesh for a filling in the new patterns, as in BML 68, 71, 84. One of the dated drafts in Luton Museum, 'Marshall May 27 1857' (Newport Pagnell) is pricked for point ground fillings. For a long time the habit of working this stitch lingered in the fingers of the lacemakers, so that they often introduced small areas of it amongst the bars and trails of the new patterns.

The tradition of a regular ground, an area of uniform mesh between the patterned head of the lace and the foot, also remained. In some of the Lester drafts and the laces made from them we can see the development of new grounds based on the plaited bars. Instead of the fine close meshes of point ground there are large open meshes worked with a varied combination of stitches. The simplest type is of plaited bars, with or without picots, worked into a square mesh, BML 43; variations of this show a small working of clothwork and clothwork with plaits at the intersections, BML 28, 35-59 (Pls 26, 29).

The finer pieces of the Lester collection show more elaborate grounds. The light trellis of the ostrich lappets (Pl. 33) has sides formed of two separately twisted pairs of threads, with picots, and a small plait at the intersections. The same ground is used in the vine border (Pl. 17). In the draft this ground is shown by

69

two parallel lines with small dots for the picots. The convolvulus flounce (Pl. 20) has a more complicated ground. The bars are plaited, with picots; along the diagonal there are alternate workings of clothwork spots and plaited webs at the intersections. These diagonals, in turn, alternate with others which have a four-petalled flower in clothwork in place of the webs, the flower having an edging of tiny loops. Some of the laces show similar work in small areas so that it appears as a filling rather than a ground. A web stitch frequently appears; in a cap, BML 58, and, with variations, in the eagle collar. It can be found worked in different ways in much of the Lester lace. The square mesh, with each side a single plait, is used mainly in borders but appears in the deep collar, BML 33 (Pl. 44) and in a narrower collar, BML 72.

The designs of the more ambitious pieces of lace are the work of a skilled and experienced hand, both in the drawing and drafting as lace patterns. These drafts and the lace made from them are well above the standard of the numerous drafts bearing the name Lester and of a large part of the lace in the collection, as well as being of a different character. Were these designs and the lace, beautifully worked from them, entirely an achievement of the Lester family and, if so, which member was responsible for the designs? In his evidence to the Commission for the Employment of Children of 1862, Thomas Lester once again voiced the lace manufacturers' complaint, as James Millward had done thirty years before,

'One great want in the trade is a school of design which would enable manufacturers to obtain patterns suitable for ordinary work. There are many French and Belgian designs but their patterns are too elaborate and difficult for the people here, and scarcely any of the manufacturers can design their own, though we do. And connected with this is a great evil in the lace trade, viz. copying of patterns which tends to discourage invention.,[34]

Amongst the items still remaining in the shop in the Arcade until Miss Haines left it were two French designs (Pl. 42). Such formal, scrolled patterns are rare in Lester lace but their influence can be seen in some pieces, for instance, in the deep collar, BML 33 (Pl. 44), and in the parchment pattern for the bonnet veil (Pl. 43).

Charles, the elder son of Thomas Lester, was already working as a partner in the firm in the 1850s and by 1862 the second son, Thomas James, had probably joined them. The catalogue entry for their 1862 exhibit is 'T. Lester & Son', but the inscription round the edge of the medal they were awarded is 'T. Lester & Sons'. If these pieces were made for either the 1862 Exhibition or the 1867 Exhibition in Paris they could be the culmination of Thomas Lester's work in the industry, but they might also be the result of his sons entering the business. Only if they were made for later exhibitions, 1873 in Vienna and 1874 in London, could they be attributed with certainty to this second generation. Style alone seems to place them between 1855 and 1875. Without other evidence any attempt at closer dating can only be tentative. There is nothing in the sketchbooks of the 1840s and the dated drafts of the 1850s designed by or for Thomas Lester which suggests the talent which produced these designs. Drawing was taught in Bedford at the Commercial School; Bradford Rudge, the Bedford artist, was drawing master there from 1840 to 1874; so tuition in drawing was available to boys of the town.[35] Nor should the women of the family be ignored. It is likely that Elizabeth Lester was a lacemaker at the time of her marriage and that she continued to add her contribution to the family business. The younger daughter, Elizabeth Sophia, might have had some training in drawing.

There is, however, no evidence which points clearly to any particular member of the family as the artist, nor any evidence to suggest the designer, or the maker, of the finest pieces in the collection.

The naturalism of these designs may have come from direct study and drawing from life. This approach had been encouraged in the Honiton industry; the hand-kerchief design by Lady Trevelyan, who worked under the influence of Ruskin, is evidence of it. The Bedfordshire lace was certainly influenced by Honiton work and the same flowers and leaves appear in both laces although the preferences and combinations are different as well as the techniques. Other contemporary laces draw on the same flower and leaf forms. The convolvulus which appears in the deep flounce, BML 9 (Pl. 20), and the handkerchief border, BML 26 (Pl. 23) also appears in Brussels lace of the same period. The convolvulus, like the fern, can also be seen in other textile designs, for example in the woven silk used for a dress of the late 1840s (Pl. 45). Nor was it limited to textile design. In an illustrated edition of Shakespeare's works, 1856—8, Lear, 'fantastically dressed with wild flowers', wears a wreath of convolvulus.

Because the English industry lacked its specialist designers, manufacturers like Thomas Lester probably relied on their own experienced eye to select designs from other sources and adapt them for lace patterns. This may be what he meant when he said, 'scarcely any of the manufacturers can design their own, though we do'. The illustrations in botanical and horticultural books of the time could have been sources, but there were also an increasing number of popular, more general periodicals which contained articles on botany and horticulture, illus-trated with steel or wood engravings and sometimes coloured plates, which could form the basis of a design. The water lily which appears in the cap, BML 59 (Pl. 29), and again in the draft for a handkerchief border, BML 377 (16) (Pl. 12), may have been derived from the many illustrations of the much-publicised Amazonian water lily, which Joseph Paxton brought to flower in the Chatsworth nurseries in 1849. It was a famous lily because of the size and structure of the leaf, which was five or six feet in diameter and so strongly veined that it could support the weight of Joseph Paxton's seven-year-old daughter. Many illustrations of this plant were published, from the most accurate botanical drawings to those issued in popular journals, like the one in the *Illustrated London News* which showed the little girl standing demurely on one of the great leaves.

Many of the women's magazines published designs for embroidery which might also have been a source of the Lester designs. From the 1850s the Lester business included Berlin woolwork which was one of the most popular forms of embroidery from the 1830s to the 1860s. Large quantities of patterns for it were imported during the 1840s. These included floral patterns, but the character of the work with its larger than life plants makes it an unlikely source. Whitework embroidery which was also popular from the beginning of the century into the 1850s needed the same delicacy of design as lace and patterns for this work were also published. Although Berlin woolwork was the only embroidery mentioned as part of the Lester business in the 1850s and 1860s, fancy work and art needlework were added to the description of the firm's range in the 1870s and 1880s.

Berlin woolwork designs were often of animals and birds. The Lester collection also has pieces which portray animals and birds worked in lace. The introduction of bird, animal and human figures into lace design was not new; they appear in lace of the seventeenth and eighteenth centuries and in the pictorial designs of some of the fan leaves of the nineteenth century. They dominate the design much more strongly in the Lester designs giving an unusual character to this lace. The sources could have been the living animals and birds drawn in the Zoological Gardens, but they are more likely to be published drawings, from a book of natural history or an illustrated article in a periodical. Sir Edwin Landseer's paintings of animals were frequently engraved and the engravings had a wide circulation. The stag of BML 20 could have been inspired by the famous *Stag at Bay*.

The rest of the collection is related in character and design to its outstanding pieces, showing the invention and ingenuity of Thomas Lester and Sons in providing patterns 'suitable for ordinary work', patterns which were within the competence of their lacemakers, and reflected the taste of the time and yet managed to keep ahead of the productions of the machines. During the 1850s the new 'Bedfordshire white fancy lace', which was Thomas Lester's own term for his work, did keep ahead but during the 1860s the Leavers machines achieved successful imitations of the Maltese-type patterns and the last advantage of the East Midlands lacemakers had gone. Yet for another forty years Charles and Thomas Lester continued to trade in hand-made lace.

The elaborate pieces surviving with their drafts and some other fine pieces were, no doubt, carefully preserved by Thomas and Charles Lester. The lesser pieces, whether kept for some special reason, or chance survivals, show the lace which must have been made in much greater quantity, small collars and cuffs and yard laces of between one and five inches wide. They share some of the characteristics of the more elaborate work. The Honiton influence is apparent in a large number of them, for instance in the collar and cuffs, BML 124, 157, 158 (Pl. 46). Floral motifs, characteristic of Devon lace are found in patterns of the Bedfordshire Maltese type BML 119-122. The raised cord in the clothwork trail and plaits laid on clothwork frequently appear, BML 15 (Pl. 41), BML 66 (Pl. 48). The treatment of linking bars and the tendency to work these into a regular mesh is characteristic, BML 22 (Pl. 47). There are examples of the simple, stereotyped patterns which were the main product of the industry in its last days like the collars, BML 76, 143, but this type of lace, generally regarded as representative of lace of the area under the name of Bedfordshire Maltese, is not dominant in this collection.

Lace Manufacturers and the Children of the Industry

By the early 1860s Thomas Lester had achieved a prominent position in the industry in Bedford and the surrounding district. The new laces he was producing were not yet having to compete with the machines; the firm had exhibited at the International Exhibition of 1862 and had been awarded a medal for the new types of lace; and in the same year Thomas Lester, the only lace manufacturer from Bedfordshire who did so, gave evidence on the industry to the Children's Employment Commission.

The Commission's concern was with the employment of children in those industries not already covered by the earlier Factory Acts, and in the lacemaking industries of the East Midlands and Devon they were particularly concerned with what was going on in the lace schools. They interviewed lace manufacturers, lace-school mistresses and children and young women who attended, or had attended, lace schools. The combined evidence of these different groups gives a detailed picture of the industry at this time of its long, slow decline.

In spite of the lower earnings from lace the number of women and children employed in the industry in the East Midlands had not fallen a great deal between 1851 and 1861 when 23,450 lacemakers were recorded for the three counties compared with 26,670 in 1851. Buckinghamshire and Northamptonshire alone account for this drop in numbers: the figures for Bedfordshire actually show a slight increase in these years, to 6,728 from 5,766. This may have been due in part to the temporary advantage given by the new laces which seem to have been adopted more extensively in Bedfordshire than in the rest of the area.

The other lace manufacturers or dealers who gave evidence to the Commissioners were all from Buckinghamshire. Thomas Gilbert, of High Wycombe, said,

'I am a pillow lace manufacturer employing lacemakers over the greater part of southern Buckinghamshire and the adjoining strip of Oxfordshire and in these districts there is no other lace manufacturer of importance. The greater part of the whole pillow lace trade is in the hands of three or four large manufacturers. I employ 3,000 persons. They are not absolutely employed by me as workpeople: but I sell them the materials, patterns and silk or thread: and there is a mutual understanding, though no legal obligation, that I should take all the lace for which I have sold patterns whether there be a demand for it or not and that the lacemakers should bring it to me and not to any other buyer. From some I buy in their own villages, travelling round for the purpose . . . In some places I do not deal directly with the lacemakers themselves, but through the agency of small buyers to whom I supply the materials and patterns and who in turn deal with the lacemakers in the same way as myself.'

The relationship of buyer and lacemaker, 'not absolutely employed by me', was the same as it had been since the earliest days of the industry in the area. What had changed was the number of lacemakers ultimately dependent on one buyer and the loss of direct contact between lacebuyer and lacemaker. This led to the intervention of another group of middlemen, 'the agency of small buyers'.

In the north of the county William Marshall of Newport Pagnell said he employed lacemakers in surrounding villages up to about fifteen miles from the town, and that he travelled to the villages to buy lace which was brought to him at the inns. This had formerly been the normal practice. He supplied patterns and parchments but, apart from black silk, the lacemakers could buy their own thread at the drapers. Another lacebuyer of Newport Pagnell, William Ayres, covered much the same area and bought lace from the smaller shops as well as direct from the lacemakers.

John Biss of Buckingham said he had been a lacedealer for twenty-four years — and a William Biss was recorded in the directories from 1830. Although he also sold what he called 'useful goods' he appeared to work in the traditional way. He supplied materials and patterns, the patterns remaining his, and he fixed beforehand the amount he would give for the complete lace, 'but the general plan is for the lacemakers to buy the pattern and material and sell their lace as their own either at local shops or to travelling buyers. The effect of this plan is to discourage a dealer from going to any expense in patterns.' Mrs Wright who in her general shop at Prestwood, near High Wycombe, also dealt in lace, said she got patterns and materials from the manufacturer and supplied them to the lacemakers, but she did not allow patterns to be seen by any but those who were working on them for that manufacturer. She was keeping, on behalf of the manufacturer, some control over his patterns. Yet the fact that a large dealer like Thomas Gilbert stated that he sold the patterns implies that this was no longer general, that much of the lace produced was from patterns in common use; and that the supply of new exclusive designs was drying up.

Some of the small buyers who worked as agents were also interviewed for the Commission. Many were local shopkeepers. Mrs Allen of High Wycombe bought 'cards and silk' from the wholesale buyers, and in turn sold the materials to the lacemakers buying lace back from them and taking the price of the materials 'out of their lace which is the custom still'. She then sold the lace to the wholesale buyers. She said that in the villages where the lace was made there might be two or three small shops who took in lace, in others none, and then the lace was taken to a shop in a neighbouring village. At these small shops the lacemakers generally had to exchange their lace for new materials, and grocery and drapery instead of money; and then,

'The shopkeepers, or "boxwomen" as they are called bring in the lace in boxes to the whole-sale buyers, from whom in turn they generally get their own grocery and drapery, etc. Some of the lacemakers who live nearer deal with the wholesale buyers direct, but on much the same plan except that a wholesale buyer makes rather more money payments, particularly if he wishes to get a large order completed quickly, and only do so when trade is good to a very small extent.'

But when a payment in money was made 'a discount is first taken off at the rate of about 1d in the 1s in the payment, with perhaps a skein of silk given in, and the rate of 6d in the £1 in payment to the boxwomen'. It was not surprising that taking off a discount by the buyer when he paid in cash made the lacemakers ' "call-out" at this more than anything'. Mrs Mobbs of Broughton, near Newport Pagnell, who had been in the business for thirty years and bought laces from the villages around, admitted that she could not now pay all in money as she used. On the other hand, the lacemakers cut off a piece of lace and brought it in to turn it into goods, 'whenever they are in want for anything for use'.

Thomas Lester said he had been in the business nearly fifty years, and

'We employ lacemakers in almost every village, and in some of these in almost every house, within a circle of 10 miles from Bedford, or more in some directions and rather less towards the south-east where the straw plait begins . . . . We purchase the lace weekly all through the year and pay in money, which we find the most advantageous and to command the best workers; and our workpeople also buy their materials of us or wherever they please. But this is only done by the chief manufacturers, others pay more or less in goods. Much lace is taken in from the makers at the shops of grocers, etc . . .'

He was still able to say in 1862; 'Improvements in machine lace do not affect the demand for this kind of lace which depends upon fashion and other accidental circumstances as the American War. Nearly a third of the whole of the lace made in Bedfordshire used to go to America and now most of this trade is stopped.'[36] By 'this lace' he was referring to 'the Bedfordshire white fancy lace in imitation of the Honiton', but the advantage the Bedfordshire lace had enjoyed was soon to come to an end, for by 1865 the Nottingham industry was successfully producing Maltese type laces by machine. William Ayres of Newport Pagnell also stated that the market for 'plait lace', by which he probably meant the lace with the mesh formed of plaits, was almost entirely confined to America.[37] This seems to be confirmed by the small quantity of such lace preserved in local collections compared with the large number of drafts pricked out for it.

What chiefly concerned the Commission was, of course, the employment of children in the industry, that is the lace schools, for the health, education and morals of the youthful poor had become an increasing weight on the conscience of the time.

The Select Committee on the Education of the Poor, looking at education in the area in 1819, when the industry was in a more flourishing state, came to the conclusion that the poor probably preferred employment to education for their children. They found many lace schools. At Marston Moretaine (population in 1801, 872) there were nine attended by about eighty to ninety boys and girls who were taught to make lace and to read, 'but very imperfectly'. Eaton Socon had only two schools, one taking ten, the other four children. Reading was taught in some schools, but generally the poorer children depended on Sunday schools for instruction in anything but lacemaking.[38] A later enquiry in 1835 found little change, although now plaiting schools were reported in some districts as well as lace schools. Maulden had six lace schools containing '36 males and 60 females at the expense of their parents', Newport Pagnell had fifteen in which two hundred and ten children made lace. At Ampthill where there were also plaiting schools, or lace and plaiting together in one school, there was an evening school, attended by those who spent the day making lace or plait.[39]

The Commission of 1843 found fewer lace schools and fewer boys attending them; and hoped that the decline of the industry would lead to their gradual disappearance, so that they would no longer prevent children from attending any other school which might be established. The Commission also saw the schools as a danger to health, places where young children worked for long hours at exacting work in unhealthy conditions. There was little difference in 1862. The schools were still

'generally the living rooms of small cottages, with the fire places stopped up to prevent draught and sometimes even in winter, the animal heat of the inmates being thought sufficient: in other cases they are small pantry-like rooms, without any fireplace; and in none of these rooms is there any ventilation beyond the door and window, the latter not always made to open, or if it will open, not opened. The crowding in these rooms and the foulness of the air produced by it are sometimes extreme. I have noticed in one place as small an amount of space as under 25 cubic feet for each person. The inmates are often exposed to the injurious effects of imperfect drains, sinks, smells, etc. common at the outsides of narrow approaches of small cottages'.

The school of Mrs Harris of Newport Pagnell was in a cottage reached by a narrow, untidy yard, the room crowded and hot. The girls were working without a candle when it was 'so dark that I could hardly see to write'. Lucy Read, aged seven, had previously been to a village school from 8 a.m. until 3.30 or 4.30 p.m. Now she worked until it was dark. She could not read and when shown a child's ABC picture book burst into tears. Jane Harris, who was eleven, had been at school five years. She had been taught to read at Sunday School.

Elizabeth Wordsworth, aged fifteen, was also at one of the Newport Pagnell schools. She said they did not read at school but that she went to night school five nights a week. However, Emma Bayley of Pytchley, who was ten years old, could read, write, read her writing and 'sum'; to prove herself she read a stanza to the commissioner, Mr. White.

The hours at the schools varied a little, but were generally 9 a.m. to 12 noon and 1 p.m. to 4 p.m. for beginners and the youngest children, now about six or seven; then after about a year 7 a.m. to 5 p.m. in winter and 8 a.m. to 8 p.m. in summer with an hour's break at midday and another break for tea for the girls who worked until 8 p.m. Often they worked even longer, 'When girls are "making up" a quantity to "cut off" and take in on Saturday they will sit up half the night to finish it as it cannot be taken unless it is an even length, or on any other day . . . Little children do not, but girls of 16 or 17 do.'

In his evidence Thomas Lester said,

'The average age of beginners may be taken at about 7; but at first they only work for a few hours perhaps 5 in a day and afterwards not 10 on average. A given quantity is set to be finished in the day and when that is done they can go . . . They soon begin to work for themselves, and by about 15 or perhaps earlier, they begin to "board themselves" at home, in which they take a pride.'

For attending the schools the fee was now 2d a week and 2½d in the winter to cover the cost of candles. Mrs Cox, lace-school mistress at Wilshampstead, added that it was 3d a week for beginners, which implies that she actually did teach the children when they first came to make lace. The average number of girls attending the lace schools was about twenty, but the number varied between twelve and twenty-five for most of the schools.

The earnings of the young children were very small. Elizabeth Emerson of Newport Pagnell had two daughters at a lace school. Charlotte, aged six, made 4d of lace in a week, and out of this 2d had to be paid for 'schooling'; her other daughter who was eight made 8d of lace but had to pay 2½d because 'she sits by candlelight'. Mrs Goodman who had a lace school at Elstow thought a girl of eight might earn 6d a week or rather more.

Mrs Emerson said her daughters suffered very much from headache. Dinah Wood, also of Newport Pagnell, spoke of the effects of lacemaking on the health of those who worked at it, 'You never see any very strong that sit at lace long . . . A good many fall into a decline and are obliged to be taken from the pillow. Black lace can hardly be seen by candlelight and working at it hurts the eyes very much and many become weak-sighted.'

In South Buckinghamshire at this time a great deal of black silk lace was made. The lace itself fetched a better price than the other laces, but the silk thread from which it was made cost much more than the cotton thread which was now in general use for most white lace. Not only was silk more expensive to buy, but its cost in proportion to the price of the lace was much higher. Elizabeth Wordsworth made two yards of black silk lace in a fortnight, worth 3s, but the buyer took 1s from this to pay for the silk. Cotton thread worked out at about 2d in the shilling, but the lace fetched far less so her earnings came to about the same in the end. Mrs Emerson confirmed these amounts for black silk lace, saying that it took fourpence in the shilling and that the silk had to be bought from the lacebuyer, 'You could not get the proper black silk at the shops, but you could get the thread for cotton lace of the same kind as the lacebuyer has only not quite so stiff, but it answers the same purpose.' The lacebuyer might then find fault with the lace if it were not made up with his own thread for, although the lacemakers believed the buyers made too much profit out of selling the thread to them, the cheaper thread from shops was possibly of poorer quality. William Marshall, a Newport Pagnell lacebuyer, said that black silk had to be bought from him, but his lacemakers were free to buy other thread where they pleased. Mrs Allen gave 3d in the shilling as the cost of the black silk, but the lacemakers were no doubt taking into account the discount that the buyer took off in addition if they were paid in cash. The making of black lace also brought extra discomfort as it was a great strain on the eyes to work at it in poor light. Mr White noticed the way the lacemakers worked round a candle stool. The candle was mounted in the centre of a stand and surrounding it were three or four flasks of water, inverted with their necks fixed into holes in the top of the stand. With only the same number of workers round the stool as there were flasks of water this was a useful device. The single candle sent refracted beams of light through each flask making a patch of strong light on the limited area of the pillow where the lace was being worked. But if there were more workers sitting round the stool than there were flasks, and in the schools this could happen, all advantage would be lost.

Border, rose and leaf design
raised work. This treatment of
petals worked as an extra layer
give a three-dimensional effect
ws the influence of the new
edlepoint lace from Belgium,
int de Gaze. The patterned
ound also has a raised effect
m the small circles of plaits
rked over the mesh of picot
s. The same treatment of the
wer heads appears in the nar-
v border, 1860–80.

BML 68

tual size.

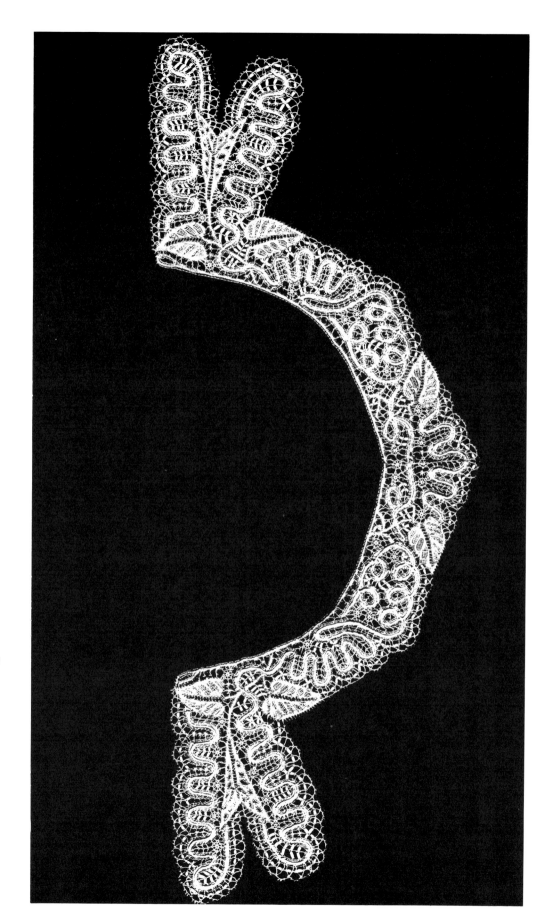

41 Collar, with basic pattern
of a corded trail in open and
closed loops, linked with bars
in a variety of stitches. The
floral spray at each tabbed
end and the leaves at the
centre back bring the influence of Honiton and the
early bobbin laces together.
Such patterns, in the smaller
pieces which were the main
production of the Lester
business, are characteristic
of the work of 1850–80.
At the back of this collar
there is a small price ticket,
10/– (10 shillings).
         BML 15
Reduced: overall length
16 1/2 in (42 cm); width
(centre back) 2 in (5 cm).

2   Two French designs for
borders, stamped: Compositeur
e Dessins pour Dentelles Ls
llard Rue Jussiennes Paris',
850–70. These were in the
op in the Arcade until
952.
uton Museum BL5/383/55
ctual size.

79

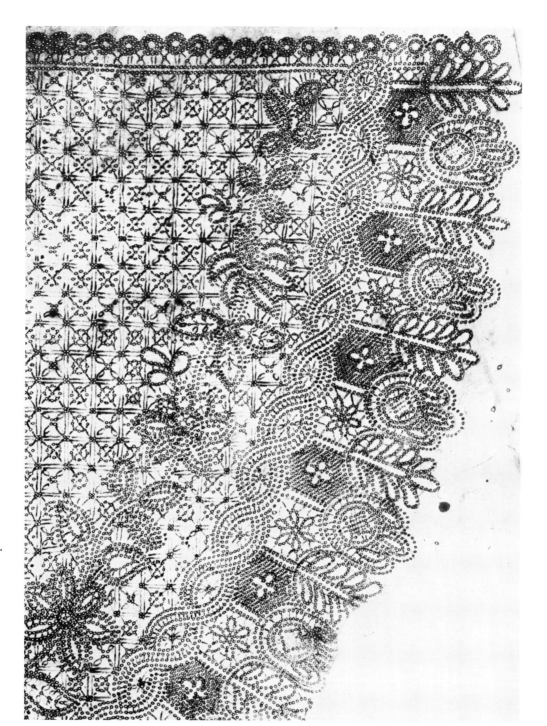

43   Part of a parchment pattern for a bonnet veil, 1855–70. The complete pattern is half of a semi-circular veil. The stylised design of the border may owe something to French designs similar to those of Pl. 42; the inner border shows a more naturalistic treatment and the ground is strongly patterned in a uniform mesh of geometric stitches.
   Luton Museum BL3/383/55
Actual size: length of veil 36 in (91 cm).

4 Deep collar with scrolled pattern in a ground of plaits worked in a square mesh; flat flower heads and leaves appear at their most stylised, keeping the outlining gimp thread, in lace with early and contemporary Italian influences, and contemporary French influence (Pl. 42) predominant, 1850—70. This fashion for a deep, falling collar on the low neckline of evening dress appeared again in the 1890s.

BML 33

Reduced: overall length 39 in (99 cm); width 9 in (23 cm).

81

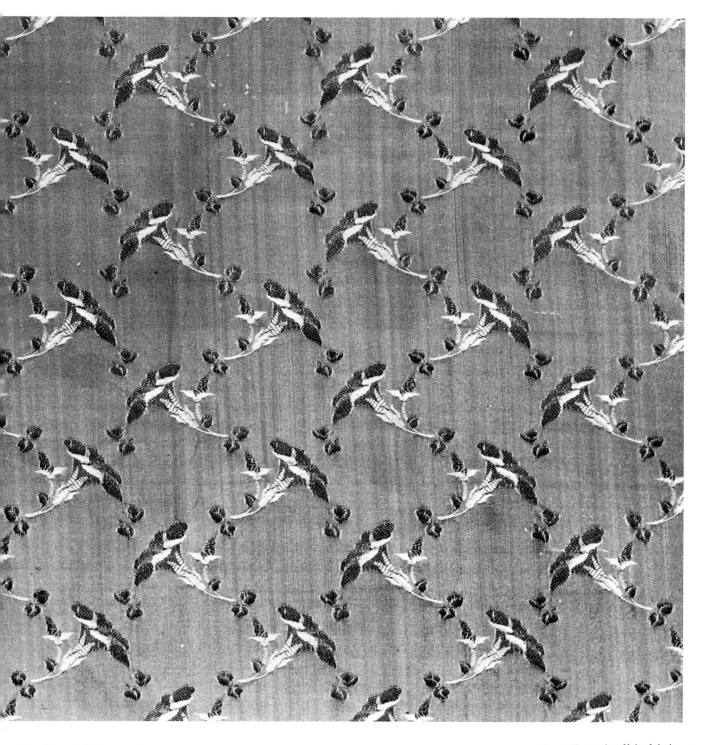

45 Figured silk in convolvulus design used for a dress
1847—9. The convolvulus
of the Lester lace designs
was, like the fern leaf, a
feature of many textile
designs of the mid-nineteenth
century.
*Manchester City Art
Galleries 1947.2295*
Actual size.

46 Collar and cuff, leaf design; ▶
not a matching set but with
the same basic pattern, a
repetitive design of two leaves
linked to form a continuous
spray. In the collar the small
bordering ground has an embossed effect from the working of small plaits at the
intersection of the plaited
bars which form a close
mesh: in the cuffs these are
worked as detached loops,
1860—80.
BML 124, 157, 158
Actual size.

The lace manufacturers were not involved in the running of the lace schools, but in some villages the lace-school mistress acted as a collector or agent for a lace dealer. This was Thomas Lester's relationship with the lace schools, which he was careful to make clear to the Commission,

'In some of the villages we have also the lace schools under our control, so far as regards the kind of lace made there and the patterns used which we supply together with the parchments, but in no other respect, the mistresses taking the scholars in their own account for a small weekly sum . . .'

Mrs Goodman of Elstow said that she took the children's lace into Bedford and brought back the money for it to pay the girls. This was probably a better arrangement than having a local shopkeeper as agent or dealer, for no truck payments were made, although the lace school mistress bought thread in bulk from the dealer for resale to the girls at the school.[40]

Receiving payments for their lace in goods not money was a serious grievance of the lacemakers. In 1862 all the buyers in Buckingham and Stony Stratford, except one, were said to pay partly in goods. This practice was not a new one. It had been so widespread in the eighteenth century that an act was passed against it in 1779. 'All persons who shall employ any lace manufacturers or shall purchase lace of them shall pay them in money and not in goods in penalty of £10 to be levied in distress.'[41] In spite of this act, in 1817 the lacemakers of Eaton Socon were complaining that they 'had great difficulty in selling lace at all without taking it out in goods in return, they cannot get ready money for their lace.'[42] The hardship caused by truck payment was greater in periods of bad trade for then payments of this kind increased. It was aggravated by the combined dealing in lace and grocery or drapery and because some of the large dealers who worked through village shops traded in this way themselves, by acting as wholesale suppliers of grocery and drapery to the smaller dealers. It was Thomas Lester's practice of always paying in money which, more than anything else, must have gained for him, and later for his sons, the respect and loyalty of those who worked for him.

The conditions of work which were seen to be harmful to the health of the lacemakers, and particularly to the children who were also lacemakers, arose not only from the work itself. Exacting work, often carried on in poor light, strained the eyes, particularly if it were in black silk; their bent and sedentary position for hours on end may have caused many ills. All these conditions were made worse for the children by the crowding together in small cottage rooms, and sometimes by the harsh discipline of a particular lace-school mistress. In theory the adult lacemakers worked what hours they pleased, but in practice necessity dictated long hours. According to some observers, and Thomas Lester was one of them, 'When there is much demand for lace and wages are high some of the girls will work very long, some as much as 16 hours for the sake of getting dress chiefly', but he was honest enough to continue, 'and others, who are forced to get a certain amount of money to support themselves may have to work twice as long to do this in a bad time as in a good.'[43]

When lace was 'good' the money women and children earned lifted the family into a modest subsistence; when lace was 'bad' this contribution became so small that fuel, food and any household comforts were severely reduced and the standard of living of many lacemaking families declined to the point of starvation. 'It would not hurt them so much,' said one woman in 1862 of the children working in the lace schools, 'if they came home to a good meal but they can get very little to eat.' From the 1840s to the 1860s the average weekly earnings of an adult lacemaker were 3s a week, and of a child 4d to 1s according to age and skill, in a district where in the family income lacemaking had for generations subsidised agricultural wages. The decline was slow: the census of 1871 still recorded 20,587 lacemakers in the three counties. The number of lacemakers in Bedfordshire was now 6,077, a drop of only a few hundred. Buckinghamshire showed a similar fall, but once again the fall was greatest, nearly two thousand, in Northamptonshire, probably because many were turning to the expanding boot and shoe industry for work.

4 The Second Generation 1870–1909

Thomas Lester died in 1867. His death was recorded in the minute book of the Bunyan Meeting, Bedford,

'Mr. Lester one of the Deacons died in the faith on 29 December 1867. He was chosen to diaconate in June 1836 and had faithfully served the church till the end of life . . . . He was a man of deeply prayerful spirit and had almost Christ-like love for little children . . . . Just before retiring he sat reading the Pilgrim's Progress . . . . before daybreak he himself passed through the gates.'[44]

In his will which he had made in 1856, he left the life interest in his estate, sworn at under £3,000, to his wife, Elizabeth. His properties were then to be shared by his four surviving children. Sarah the elder daughter, married to Thomas Emery received one property in Tavistock Street; the younger son Thomas James the other. Elizabeth the younger daughter had the house in Dame Alice Street; and the High Street premises, 'in his own occupation, in part of which I and my said son Charles Fox Lester now carry on business', was left to Charles, the elder son. Everything else was to be sold and, apart from legacies to the children, all went to his wife. The stock of the business was also to be sold, but 'If the said Charles Fox Lester desire to take over the whole business now carried on by me and himself in partnership he can do so, taking over the house in High Street at £45 per annum rent.'[45]

Thomas James Lester was probably already in the business at the time of his father's death, although apparently not also in partnership at the time the will was made. Immediately afterwards the business became C. & T. Lester, recorded in the Post Office directory of 1869, 'C. & T. Lester, lace manufacturers, Berlin Wool repository, 99 High Street'. The first hint of dealing in materials other than lace was in the entry in Craven's Directory of 1854, 'T. Lester & Son, lace manufacturers and Berlin Wool repository'. By 1877 the business had moved to 115 High Street (Pl. 49).

C. & T. Lester exhibited at the Vienna exhibition of 1873 and were awarded a medal 'for merit' in Class V (Textiles and Clothes) in the section devoted to 'Lace net, lace dresses, curtains, etc'. They also exhibited in the following year in the London International Exhibition where they again received a medal in Class VIII. Mrs Bury Pallister wrote a review of the lace exhibition there for the *Art Journal.* After praising the Honiton work exhibited by Howell and James and the reproductions of old work by Mrs Treadwin of Exeter,

'We would also direct attention to the Bedford lace exhibited by Mr. Lester, most praiseworthy for its beautiful workmanship. A kind of cordonnet is laid on with wonderful firmness and the even weaving of the leaves is remarkable. Mr. Lester has great merit in keeping up the standard of the industry as the workers are too prone to prefer working at the Cluny and Maltese laces which spoil their fingers for more delicate work.'[46]

Mrs Palliser repeated her commendation of Mr Lester's lace in the 1875 edition of her *History of Lace,* a tribute which was edited out of the subsequent edition of 1902, which has since been the standard edition of her work. *The Queen* also had a word of praise for the Lester lace, 'As a meritorious attempt to improve the English humdrum laces, we must mention the exhibit of Mr C. T. Lester [sic] of Bedford. His case would have well deserved a place in the principal room, instead of being banished amongst the Nottingham loom laces.'[47]

Charles and Thomas Lester could still in the 1870s draw on sufficient skill amongst their lacemakers to produce lace of fine workmanship. Recollections of lacemakers who were still living in the 1940s reveal the running of the Lester business in the late nineteenth century. Most of the Bedfordshire lacemakers remembered making lace for Lester, although there were also references by Stevington lacemakers to Mr Harker and Mr Rabans, both of Stevington; Mr Harker afterwards moved to Bedford, where he described himself as 'designer and pillow lace manufacturer'. Amongst parchment patterns in Northampton Museum, said to have belonged to Mr Harker, D. 133/1964, there is one for a plastron, a trimming added to the front of the bodice, fashionable in the 1880s. This is of Bedfordshire Maltese type lace and is stamped with a monogram $c^{\&}_{L}T$. The stamp of C. and T. Lester on other parchments, at Luton and Bedford, is not in this form. In 1877 there were still four other dealers in Bedford; only one of them, J. Hornsey, who had been there since the 1850s, was long established. There were four other dealers in the county, at Cranfield, Kempston, Ampthill and Turvey. Lacemakers at Harrold and Riseley also sold to Miss Savage, the general shopkeeper in Riseley who often paid in goods. Other Bedford lacebuyers mentioned were Braggins, the drapers, who have an almost unbroken record of dealing in lace and lacemaking since first established in Bedford, until 1980. Other Bedford drapers dealing in lace were E. P. Rose and T. Coombs. But so long as Thomas Lester was in business most of the lace was made for him.

Mrs Hulatt, born in 1869, remembered the two brothers touring the villages 'in a fly', and visiting her village, Radwell, once a month. The parchments she had from them were on loan and stamped with their name. Mrs Dawson also spoke of the Lesters' monthly visit to Willington, although later the visits came to an end and the lacemakers had to take their lace into Bedford. Mrs Bowyer of Stevington remembered doing this, walking into Bedford to sell her lace.

Some villages had a local collector. Mrs Pettit of Great Barford collected lace from the Roxton lacemakers and took it into Bedford for sale every Saturday. In Wilden, Mr Cave, born in 1876, 'ran round to Mrs Draper's' with his mother's lace, so that Mrs Draper could take it into Bedford. Mrs Webb, born in 1861, remembered Miss Gasking coming round once a month to a cottage in Odell to collect the village lace. John Gasking was a Turvey dealer of the 1860s and 1870s. Later Mrs Webb sold to Lester taking her lace from Willington to the shop in High Street. She recalled the glass roof in the shop where Mr Lester took the lace to inspect it in a good light. She confirmed what Mrs Hulatt said of the Lester patterns, that they were on loan and had to be returned with the finished lace. She added that there were special lacemakers scattered throughout the villages who worked the more elaborate and difficult patterns and these workers were well paid and often had their pay advanced. Thomas Lester's statement that he always paid in money not in goods was confirmed by the lacemakers; and that he paid a good price for good work and was critical of the quality and workmanship of lace brought to him. The Lesters had the custom of presenting a bobbin to a worker in recognition of a specially good piece of work. Mrs Swannell, born in 1860, received one of these when she was about thirteen. She recalled standing by 'Lester's cart' when he noticed her lace, 'This is yours, is it?', then looking at it said, 'You've made your lace so well, young 'un, so I'll give you a bobbin'. This bobbin, now inscribed: 'A gift from Lester' is in the Bagshawe collection, Luton Museum. Mrs Hulatt also received a bobbin, now in the same collection, but hers is a plain one. Probably Lester would give a plain bobbin and the lacemaker commemorate the gift by having it inscribed.

Mrs Dawson reckoned that working eight and a half hours she could earn 4d a day for a Bedfordshire Maltese edging. Mrs Armstrong, born in 1860, at Thurleigh, said (1943) that in her prime she could work about a yard and a half of a Bedfordshire Maltese border, one and a half inches wide, in two days. For this Lester would pay her 1s 6d a yard, so that for a full week's work she might earn six or seven shillings. This was more than double Mrs Dawson's earnings and much higher than the earnings usually quoted, 4d to 6d a day, so Mrs Armstrong was probably making good quality lace.[48]

The lace made by these lacemakers was of the Bedfordshire Maltese type, although several remembered their mothers or grandmothers making point ground lace. By the 1870s these laces too were being produced by machine and the hand-made lace industry turned to even simpler laces in the effort to evade machine competition. Torchon, an unsophisticated lace of repetitive geometric patterns based on diagonals, with a heavy, five-hole mesh, was made and 'Yak' lace, similar in pattern to torchon or Bedfordshire Maltese, but worked with a worsted thread, in black or cream. But by the 1890s torchon too was being produced as a machine-made lace.

C. and T. Lester now no longer relied entirely on lace for their business. They advertised in *The Bedford Bee,* 1879, as 'Messrs C. & T. Lester, Berlin and Fancy Warehouse, Lace Manufacturers', and in a local publication, *Where to Buy: Town and Trade of Bedford* c. 1891, the High Street shop is illustrated (Pl. 49) and the business described as, 'Manufacturers and Designers of Real Lace and Art Needlework Warehouse'. In 1893 they exhibited at the Chicago Exhibition, and soon after this issued a trade card with the full list of their exhibition awards (Pl. 50b). Two pieces sent to Chicago are in the Cecil Higgins Art Gallery, BML 339, 340 (Pls 51, 52); the lace is similar in character to the Honiton-influenced pieces, but not of the quality of the best of these. The collar, BML 340 (Pl. 52), is identical with another in the collection, BML 102. Writing of English lace at this exhibition, Florence F. Miller said, 'Some charming Honiton lace and coarser pillow laces from Bucks and various other parts of England; but the latter can never compete with machine-made lace, the resemblance being so close in all points except price.'[49]

The design of these late exhibition pieces shows a great falling off from the lace which was probably sent to earlier exhibitions, and from the lace commented on with approval by Mrs Palliser in 1874. The quality of design throughout the collection is uneven, in both the more ambitious and the simpler laces. A deep flounce, BML 8, ambitious enough in size, shows a coarsening of design and workmanship from the flounce, BML 9 (Pl. 20), which was probably its inspiration. A debased form of acorn design worked in coarse thread appears in a cap, BML 39, similar in shape to BML 43. A collar of Honiton type lace with an acorn design shows weakness of workmanship as well as design, BML 105 (Pl. 53). On the other hand, there are small collars of simple attractive patterns, BML 115, delicately worked in a trellis with groups of plaits laid on clothwork, and BML 78 which has fillings of the same fine square mesh with grouped picots as BML 66 (Pl. 48) and BML 142. Two collars, BML 15 and BML 138 (Pls 41, 54), show the range of quality in design and workmanship in a single type of Lester lace.

These may measure the decline in the quality of the Lester lace in general with the decline of the industry, just as the Chicago exhibition pieces reflect a decline from the finest pieces in the collection, but it is likely that at all times the Lester business included a range of quality in the lace bought and sold and poor design and workmanship may not always be a sign of lace of 1890–1910.

The number employed in the East Midlands was now falling rapidly. The census of 1881 recorded 12,480 in the three counties. The drop in Bedfordshire was still less than in the other two counties: just under five thousand people worked in lace in a county of over a hundred and fifty thousand inhabitants. But during the next ten years the industry declined almost to extinction. The total number for all three counties in 1891 was down to 3,376.

The End of the Lace Schools

Most of the lacemakers still left in the industry by 1890 were middle-aged or elderly. The lace schools had at last crumbled under the pressure of two move-ments of social change. The employment of children in industry had already been controlled; control was extended to handicrafts by the Workshops Act of 1867. This Act stated that no child under eight was to be employed in any handicraft and children of eight to thirteen for half-time only. It made no exception for children employed by their parents so that it should have excluded all children under eight from lace schools and halved the hours of attendance for those be-tween eight and thirteen. But the provisions for enforcement were inadequate and the fact that a dwelling house in which none but the inmates worked was outside the Act made it possible for small groups of children still to gather in 'family' groups in a cottage. Mrs Armstrong of Thurleigh said she 'picked up' lacemaking at the age of six and then went with four or five other children to a neighbour's house. They went at 8 a.m. and stayed till the work was done. This would have been happening in the year of the Act and a few years afterwards, but it was bound to take some time for parents in the lacemaking villages to discover that such old ways were now illegal. Mrs Swannell, who like Mrs Armstrong was born in 1860, went to a lace school in Felmersham, with about twenty girls between eight and twelve years old, so the age restriction of the 1867 Act was being ob-served there. But the school lasted from 8 a.m. till 6 p.m. with an hour for dinner and an hour for tea. They used candlestools, a stool with four flasks for four children, the proper way. She had to repeat a text from the Bible before she left each evening and one girl had to stay to sweep up the room. They paid the lace-school mistress 3d a week. The worst punishment was to be made to stay behind and work another head of lace.[50]

The movement towards a national system of elementary education for all chil-dren added its pressure to that of the Workshops Act. From the beginning of the century there had been growing concern about the education of the poor, which was haphazard, dependent on charity schools, village schools run by local clergy or landowners and a few independent ventures. In 1819 it was reported that in Goldington, 'The poor are without sufficient means of education, and owing to the children being employed in lacemaking would not be able to avail themselves

9   a. Shop of C. and T. Lester,
15 High Street, Bedford, c. 1890.
. The site today, now occupied
y the Midland Bank Ltd.

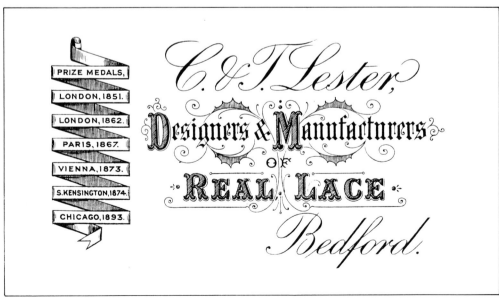

50   a. Thomas James Lester,
1834–1909, c. 1900.
b. Trade card of C. and T. Lester,
c. 1895 – 1900.

51   Collar, rose design,
exhibited at the Chicago
Exhibition, 1893, based on
elements of earlier patterns
of Honiton type.
        BML 339
Reduced: length (outer edge
26 in (66 cm); width (corners) 3 in (7.6 cm).

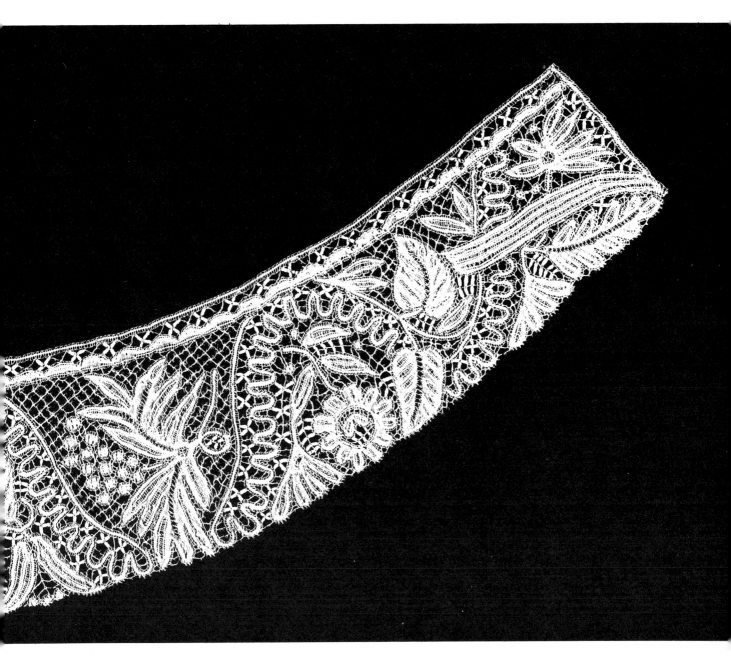

2   Collar, flower, leaf and
erry design, exhibited at the
hicago Exhibition, 1893.
ased on elements of earlier
atterns, but showing little
ttempt to design for the
ollar shape, each end being
nished by an edging and
ot treated as part of the
esign.
BML 340
educed: length 39 in
9 cm); width 3 1/4 in
.3 cm).

53   Collar, acorn design,   ►
Honiton type pattern, show-
ing decline in design and
execution, 1880—1900.
BML 105
Actual size.

95

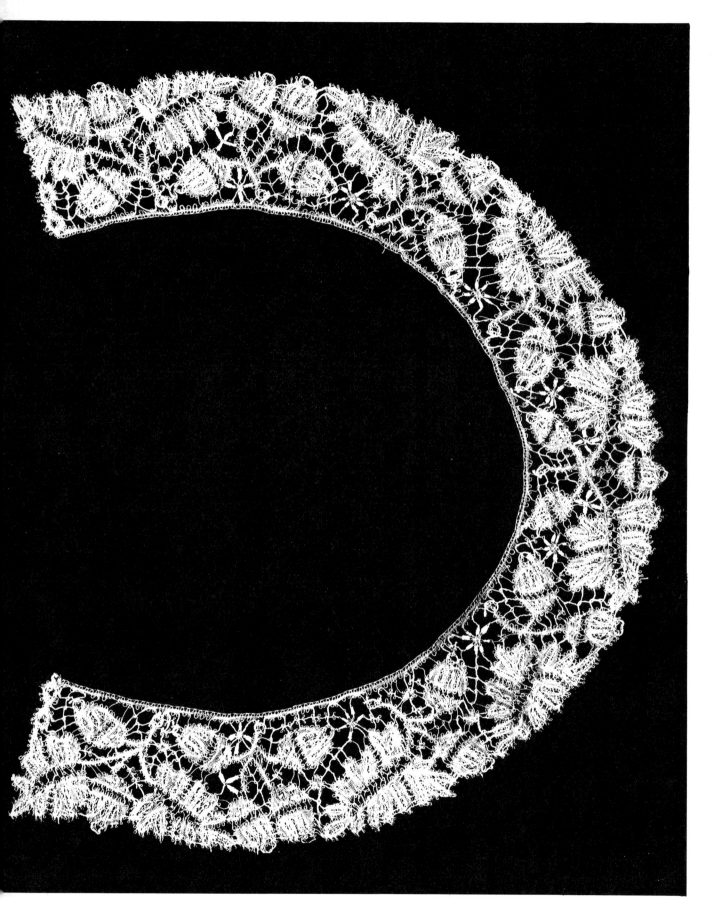

97

of instruction except on Sundays.'[51] Since the end of the eighteenth century the Sunday schools were attempting to make good the lack of any other education for children of the poor. Where there were no day schools for them it is hardly surprising that the lace schools developed in the lacemaking district, to train the children to earn a living. At this time various religious denominations were setting up schools and between them they received the first government grant, £20,000 for the whole country, in 1883. By 1846 the Established Church, through its National Society, had set up schools in many villages, but there were still villages without a school other than a lace or plaiting school and a Sunday school. The existence of the lace or plaiting schools probably discouraged the setting up of a voluntary school. In a survey made by the National Society in 1846 it was reported from Keysoe, that there was 'great difficulty in keeping a school together – the children were all brought up to lacemaking.' The schools were run on voluntary contributions, a small annual grant from the government and the fees paid by the children, usually 2d a week. They were not always well attended because families needed the extra money that children could earn by their lacemaking, small as the amounts were. Although the state supported and supervised the voluntary provision of education, it was obvious by 1870 that this was inadequate and uncertain and was still undermined by the long tradition of child labour. An act was passed which for the first time made the provision of standard basic education the responsibility of the state. New schools were built and some voluntary schools handed over to the new school boards which were elected locally to administer local education, with powers to levy a rate to maintain the service. Parents who could afford it were still expected to contribute a small weekly attendance fee for each child.[52]

In a report, made in 1876, on the working of the Workshops Regulation Act, an inspector visiting the area welcomed the dwindling away of the lace schools, but thought that if the Act were enforced to the letter it would lead to the end of the hand-made industry. He suggested that for a short period each day the children over six years of age should be allowed to carry on lacemaking at the new schools. This would he thought

'keep those abominations, the plait and pillow-lace schools (a few of which despite the Workshops Acts still linger about the country) out of the field. The work itself, if not extended over too long a time, is not hard even for the smallest children. If, for instance, a maximum of one hour a day were fixed for a child under seven, two hours for a child under eight, three for a child under nine, four for a child under ten, it would be no hardship to the child and a great benefit to the parents.'[53]

The suggestions of the inspector were not officially adopted and although lacemaking still appeared amongst other subjects in some voluntary schools, even this limited survival was actively discouraged. There were now evening lace schools which girls attended after their day at the new schools, thus reversing the situation at Ampthill in the 1830s when they attended lace schools by day and night schools for general education. Mrs Webb, born at Odell, remembered (1943) going to one of these evening schools after a day school.

The Workshops Act of 1867 and the Education Act were the pressures from without which helped to close the lace schools, but before any legislation protected the children from long hours of work in crowded cottage rooms, or provided them with general education, lace schools were closing as the industry declined. Already in 1862 Thomas Lester thought there were more children working at home than in the lace schools, and although he used the lace schools, 'As a general rule we prefer those who have been taught at home to those who have been

54 Collar with corded trail and flat flower-head design, showing decline in design and execution compared with collar in the same type of lace, BML 15 (Pl. 41), 1880–1900.

BML 138

Actual size.

98

amongst a large number at school, and we find them better workers.' Thomas Lester was deeply involved with the Sunday schools of the Baptist Church and spoke of the influence of the Sunday schools in his evidence, 'The influence of this teaching extends to the general conduct of the people in the week and is shown by their more orderly and refined behaviour, for instance when the girls bring their work in to be sold.'[54]

Most of the generation of lacemakers born after 1870, the last generation to experience lacemaking as an industry, were taught or 'picked up' lacemaking at home. Mrs Cave, born in 1877 at Wilden, the daughter of a lacemaker, did the housework while her mother made lace, and then at the age of fourteen was taught by an aunt who had herself started at the age of six. Mrs Dawson of Willington learnt from her sister-in-law when she was eight, although she remembered a lace school at Willington and said that Mrs Langley who kept it did teach the children how to make lace. In 1943 Mrs Dawson could still remember her sister-in-law's instructions, 'pull the chain up tight' and 'plenty of twists in the footside'. Like most of her generation the lace she learnt to make was the Bedfordshire Maltese type.

The Lace Associations

In 1891, when the industry was on the point of disappearing, the Department of Science and Art at last took note of its problems; and its undermining weakness and need which James Millward had diagnosed in 1835 and Thomas Lester had emphasised again in 1862. The English lacemakers did not lack skill, 'English lacemakers are skilled, work thread and silk easily and produce work of excellent quality'. This was the comment of the French jurors of the 1867 Paris Exhibition. In 1891 A. S. Cole visited the three counties to report on the possibility of improving and developing the industry by technical instruction in design and the application of design to practical lacemaking. Calling at Ridgmont he examined the work of lacemakers there and found that 'No patterns of any importance have been supplied to the workers here for fifty years. Dealers have given out patterns for small borders and edgings'. Many lacemakers pricked off their own patterns from lace. He found 6d a day was considered good earnings. Although he thought lacemaking might be treated as a subject of technical instruction in schools, his conclusion was as discouraging as it was realistic;

'Commercial influence is insufficient to foster the higher possibilities of lace-making; as commercial influence in England arises from the commerical working of supply and demand, differing therefore in character and quality from the commercial influence in France, which is flavoured with artistic taste and perception of the value of technical instructions.'[55]

Mr Cole's report produced no official response, but there was now a new element in the industry. Some of the nobility and gentry of the three counties became aware of the effect its decline was having on the income of their poorer neighbours and realised that an established local craft of some beauty and skill was about to be lost. Patronage of the industry by buying its products was nothing new, but now there was to be closer involvement. In 1891, just before Mr Cole made his visit, an exhibition of lace was held at Northampton to awaken interest and increase its sales. From this the Midlands Lace Association was set up as a permanent organisation for collecting and selling lace for the lacemakers at a better price than they could get from the dealers. The Association at first worked from a depot in Adnitts store, the Northampton drapers, and Mr Cole was told that the prices given for lace by buyers had improved a little following the exhibition. Members of the working committee, all ladies who had been interested in lacemaking in their own villages, worked as collectors and distributors.

The Midlands Association worked mainly in the Northampton area. In 1897 another Association was formed, the North Buckinghamshire Lace Association which later, to bring in Bedfordshire, became the Buckinghamshire (North Buckinghamshire and Bedfordshire) Association with an imposing list of royal patrons and titled vice-presidents. It had two aims; to sell the lacemakers' work direct from maker to purchaser to secure 'an adequate return for skilled labour and saving the large profits made in all trades by the middlemen'; and to encourage the making of better quality lace, particularly the point ground lace traditional to the area. At the London Exhibition of 1874 it was noted 'Of Buckinghamshire lace we failed to find a single specimen.'[56] By this time the term Buckinghamshire lace generally meant point ground lace, and Bedfordshire lace all types of East Midlands lace without ground, as exemplified in the Lester Collection. Later, Bedfordshire lace usually meant only Bedfordshire Maltese lace. The Association ambitiously set up a London depot, but the habit of private sales by the ladies of the Association amongst their friends, worked against a realistic organisation for the wider marketing of the lace, although it brought immediate advantage to the lacemakers in better prices, at least to those who could still make point ground lace and lace of high quality.[55]

One of the effects of the decline, as standards of design and execution were lowered, had been a general loss of discrimination amongst private buyers. Those who wore hand-made lace tended to buy lace of high quality, Chantilly and, towards the end of the century, a new type of needlepoint lace, *Point de Gaze.* Even the narrower laces of Valenciennes, which had a wide range of quality in the nineteenth century, were used instead of the comparable laces of the East Midlands. Those who had formerly bought East Midlands lace had turned to many varieties of lace constantly produced by the machine-lace industry. When lace, after being less in evidence in the 1880s, appeared in some quantity on underwear as well as dress in the 1890s, most of it was machine-made and little advantage came to the East Midlands. The Association had to work to create new markets.

Many of the older lacemakers still had parchments pricked with the fine point ground patterns they had worked in their youth (Pl. 13). Now when the opportunity came to work from them again, ageing sight and lack of practice often made the finer, complicated patterns beyond their powers. The Associations searched for patterns of good design, collected and preserved them, but they recognised the need for new designs, reflecting current taste.[57] They faced the same problem which had hampered the industry for many years, and designing lace patterns proved more difficult than many members of the Association realised. Miss Effie Bruce-Clarke, a member of the Midlands Association's working committee, who published many articles on lace and on the Association's work, wrote in the *Art Journal,* 1896,

'Patterns promulgated by those in high places have been tried and found wanting. The half-educated worker with her art at her elbow knows her lace and her 'piller' and its difficulties as an art student puffed with pride and prizes but ignorant of technique can never do.'[58]

and quoted a lacemaker's response to one of these patterns, ' "There aint owt to start yer downs from in pattern" '. She found many of the lacemakers skilled in design as it related to their work. Lord Ernle met similar knowledge and understanding in a lacemaker at Oakley a few years later,

100

'An elderly woman, named Curtis, the wife of the roadman, was a skilled maker of point ground lace. During my tramps through France I had gone out of my way to visit Alençon where in 1880 lace-making was still a cottage industry, and had bought three yards from one of the peasant workers. When I showed this fabric to Mrs. Curtis . . . . she surprised me by her intelligent comparison of her work with that of her French rival. She told me also that she never had any difficulty in finding customers for her products. The disappearance of such an industry seemed another symptom of the decay of village life. To revive it would be to restore a lost interest, increase earning power, and renew the refining influence of the practice of an artistic craft. For these reasons therefore, in October 1906, I supported an application from a Bedfordshire village for financial assistance in starting a lace class.' [59]

This was the beginning of another organisation, the Bedfordshire Lace Education Committee, whose aim was to provide instruction in the making of point ground lace for the children in the county and to carry on the making of lace for the next generation. Classes were to be held in the villages, outside school hours, but with some financial help, through small grants, from the County Council. The Committee built up a collection of parchments of good design and supplied suitable thread. The pupils sold lace privately, to the Associations or to local shops still dealing in lace. The Committee's chief problem was finding teachers for its classes. In 1924 its work came to an end when the Board of Education changed its policy of authorising grants to voluntary bodies for handicraft classes, although lace-making was allowed for a period of not more than one hour a week in elementary schools. Between 1924 and 1930 nine schools in Bedfordshire included lace-making in their curriculum, but the difficulty of finding teaching staff who could also teach lacemaking reduced the number to four by 1930,

'In view of the small number of schools in which it has been found possible to carry out instruction in lacemaking, the lack of teachers, and the results obtained, it is doubtful if the continuation of this instruction in schools in which it is now taught or its introduction into Central Schools when they are established is warranted.' [60]

The Lace Associations found no difficulty in selling point ground lace. They revived interest in it and created a demand for it. They also helped to raise a little the rates of payment for good quality lace. But they could not revive an industry so far declined. During the 1920s the Associations declined also. The lace dealers they thought they might replace to the benefit of the lacemakers had also disappeared one by one, leaving only the draper-lace dealers or the art needlework-lace dealers to buy and sell an uncertain supply of lace.

The Last Years

The Lace Associations gathered in some of the better lacemakers and after 1900 were taking the place of dealers, but in the 1890s the Midlands Lace Association worked mainly outside the Bedford area, and the North Buckinghamshire Association was not formed until 1897, so the Lester business may not have been greatly affected. Charles Lester had died in 1885 and from 1897 Miss Elizabeth Driver appears as partner in the firm, now Lester and Driver. Thomas Lester retired in 1903, but the name Lester and Driver, Lace Warehouse was kept not only until his death in 1909, but until Miss Florence Haines took over the business in 1913.

Charles Fox Lester, the elder brother, remains a rather shadowy figure. It is possible that he was responsible for the needlework side of the business, as the addition of 'Berlin woolwork repository' to its description coincides with its becoming 'T. Lester and Son' instead of 'T. Lester', and it was this side of the business that Miss Driver took over. Charles Lester became a trustee of the Bunyan

Meeting, as his father had been, in 1876.[61] Lacemakers' memories often seemed a composite memory of the two brothers, distinguished only by the hope that it would be Thomas who came to take the lace they had brought to the shop, because he tended to give slightly higher prices than his brother.[62]

The family followed their father in active support of the Baptist Church. In 1884 Thomas Lester and his sister Elizabeth gave the chains and posts to mark the right-of-way to the branch church at Goldington. In 1902 Miss Lester gave a piece of land at the rear of the church for the building of a classroom and kitchen.[63] She was a partner in her brother's business dealings outside the lace trade. They jointly had a financial interest of £6,000 in the Swan Hotel.[64]

By 1898 Thomas Lester had left the house which had been designed for him by John Usher, a Bedford architect, where he had lived since 1869 and which still stands, Holly Lodge, 43, The Grove. He went to live at Kimbrook House, Stonely, Kimbolton where he died, aged seventy-five, on 22 November 1909.[65] His obituary in the *Bedfordshire Times* of 26 November stated that the business had been begun by his father in 1811, when the first Thomas, or Thomazin, Lester would have been twenty years old. This was probably family knowledge, which sets the date earlier than any record traced so far. It says of Thomas James Lester,

'He took a keen interest in the manufacture of real lace and by constantly producing new designs did more than any one else had done or could do to keep the industry alive. In earlier years he was very successful in gaining medals and certificates of merit at all the principal exhibitions both at home and abroad, for beauty of design and excellence of manufacture.'

He left a net estate of over £20,000 to his two surviving, unmarried daughters and his late wife's sister, who was living with the family in the early days at Holly Lodge. By the terms of the will the High Street premises were sold.[66] The Lester and Driver business moved to 6, The Arcade where it remained, still dealing in a little lace, but mainly an art needlework business. When Miss Haines took over in 1913, it became an art needlework business by name, although Miss Haines still dealt in a small trickle of lace.

For the craft did not die. The Lace Associations were weakened by the First World War, 1914 to 1918, and the new ways of the 1920s broke them altogether. Lacemaking, at its lowest ebb in the 1930s, was briefly stimulated when American airmen arrived in the district during the Second World War, and bought lace to send home. During the 1950s a few enthusiasts re-awakened interest, learning lacemaking as a craft for their own times; and the movement they started has grown. Now, with the full approval of educational authority, it flourishes, no longer a cottage industry for the poor, but a craft of leisure for a more fortunate generation.

References

Note Parliamentary papers are referred to in the notes by Commons session and volume number, thus: PP (1819), IXA.

1. *Journal of the House of Lords,* XXXVI (30 June 1780).
2. Proceedings of the Committee of Lace Manufacturers for the Counties of Buckingham, Bedford and Northampton, 1814—6, MS., Cowper and Newton Museum, Olney.
   59 Geo. III c. 52.
3. *The Wynne Diaries,* Edited by Anne Fremantle (London, 1935—40), vol. III (1940), p. 291.
4. *Calendar of Treasury Papers,* CCVIII, no. 47.
5. *Universal British Directory of Trade and Commerce* (London, 1790).
   Licence issued to John Coleman in Cecil Higgins Art Gallery, Bedford.
6. C.C. Channer, *Practical Lacemaking,* p. 6.
7. *Some Considerations humbly offered to the honourable House of Commons, concerning the Proposed Repeal of an Act lately Passed to render the Laws Prohibiting the Importation of Foreign Bone Lace &c more Effectual* (London? 1698). Pamphlet; copy in Victoria and Albert Museum.
8. A. Young (ed.), *Annals of Agriculture,* vol. XXXV (1800), p. 171; vol. XXXVII (1801), p. 448.
9. Select Committee on the Education of the Poor, PP (1819), IXA, pp. 1—14, Digest of returns, Bedfordshire.
10. Beds. County Record Office, BY 1/2, pp. 41, 48; BY 17/1; St Paul's Parish Register.
11. *Northampton Mercury,* 4 September 1830.
12. *Journal of the House of Lords,* XXXVI (30 June 1780); *Journal of the House of Commons,* XIII (6 March 1699).
13. *Report of the Select Committee on Arts and Manufacturers, Part II,* PP (1836), IX, pp. 16—20.
14. *Art Journal: The Illustrated Catalogue of the International Exhibition Paris, 1867* (London, 1868), p. 116.
15. Ornamental Design Act, 1842; Public Record Office, Registers, BT 44.31.
16. 6 Geo. IV c. 111; 5 & 6 Vic. c. 47; 9 & 10 Vic. c. 23; 23 & 24 Vic. c. 110.
17. Select Committee on the Poor Law Amendment Act. PP (1837—8), XVIII, Ampthill Union.
18. *Second Report of the Commissioners for inquiring into the Employment of Children,* PP (1843), XIV, pp. A12, 50—6.
19. Photographs in A. A. Carnes Collection, Somerset County Museum.

20. J. Donaldson, *General View of the Agriculture of the County of Northampton* (Edinburgh, 1794);
T. Batchelor, *General View of the Agriculture of the County of Bedford,* (London, 1808).

21. *Second Report of the Commissioners for inquiring into the Employment of Children,* PP (1843), XIV, p. A12.

22. *Bedfordshire Times,* 10 May 1912. Contribution by R. Haskins, grandson of J. Haskins, beadmaker, Ampthill Street; *Pigot's Directory,* 1839.

23. For more detailed and illustrated classification of bobbins and other lace-making equipment, see C. E. Freeman, *Pillow Lace in the East Midlands,* (Luton Museum and Art Gallery, 1958).
Luton Museum, the Cecil Higgins Art Gallery and Bedford Museum all have examples of the inscribed Lester bobbins.

24. Beds. County Record Office, BY 1/2, January 30 1868.

25. C. C. Channer, *Practical Lacemaking,* pp. 67—72.

26. Stevington Baptist Church Minute Book. Note on the death of J. Roberson, 1835.

27. Exhibition of the Works of Industry of All Nations, 1851, *Official Catalogue* (London, 1851), Thomas Lester entry no. 236, class XIX; *Reports by the Juries* (London, 1852), pp. 560, 568, 571, 573.

28. T. Wright, *The Romance of the Lace Pillow,* pl. 27.

29. Exhibition of 1851, *Supplementary Report on Design,* p. 747.

30. International Exhibition, 1862. *Jurors' Reports,* class XXIV, English Pillow Lace, p.3.

31. P. Wardle, *Victorian Lace,* p. 152, fig. 8.

32. Exhibition of 1851, *Supplementary Report on Design,* p. 747.

33. *First Report of the Commissioners on the Employment of Children,* 1862, PP (1863), XVIII, p. 262.

34. *Ibid.*

35. J. Godber, *The Harpur Trust, 1552—1973* (Bedford, 1973), pp. 72, 81.

36. *First Report of the Commissioners on the Employment of Children,* pp. 256—62.

37. F. W. Bull, *History of Newport Pagnell* (1900), Account of lace trade supplied by W. Ayres, lace merchant, p. 196.

38. Select Committee on the Education of the Poor, PP (1819), IXA, pp. 1—14, Digest of Returns, Bedfordshire.

39. *Abstract of Answers and Returns relative to the State of Education in England and Wales,* PP (1835), XLI.

40. *First Report of the Commissioners on the Employment of Children,* 1862, pp. 185, 256—62.

41. 17 Geo. III c. 49.

42. Lords Committee on the Poor Laws, 1817, PP (1818), V, p. 162.

43. *First Report of the Commission on the Employment of Children,* 1862, p. 262.

44. Beds. County Record Office, BY 1/2, January 30 1868.

45. Beds. County Record Office, CC 318.

46. *Art Journal,* N.S. XIII (1874), p. 173.

47. *The Queen,* 18 April 1874, p. 325.

48. Information collected from Mrs Armstrong, Cave, Dawson and Webb by the author, 1943; from Mrs Bowyer, Hulatt and Livett (Roxton) by the late Mr T. W. Bagshawe, 1948—9. I am indebted to his sons, Mr Richard and Mr Nicholas Bagshawe for allowing me access to their father's notes and permis-

sion to quote from them.

49. *Art Journal* (1893). Supplement, *The Chicago Exhibition.*
     Not surprisingly, there is no record of an award for the lace exhibited at
     Chicago. The prize medal awarded in 1851 was the second category of
     award: at the 1862 Exhibition there were two categories, medals and
     commendations; Thomas Lester was awarded a medal. The medal from the
     Paris Exhibition of 1867 was a bronze medal, the third category there. From
     Vienna the medal was of the fifth category, 'for merit'. The 1874 medal was
     one given to all exhibitors. I am indebted to Mr James Graham for his help
     in checking the exact categories of the awards represented by the medals in
     the Lester collection.
50. Bedfordshire Women's Institutes, *Year Book* (1949).
51. Select Committee on the Education of the Poor, PP (1819), IXA, pp. 1—14,
     Digest of Returns, Bedfordshire.
52. J. Godber, *History of Bedfordshire, 1066—1888* (Bedford, 1969), pp. 506—7,
     541.
53. *Report of the Commissioners to Inquire into the Working of the Factory and
     Workshops Acts,* PP (1876), XXIX, App. C, p. 86.
54. *First Report of the Commissioners on the Employment on Children,* 1862,
     p. 262.
55. Alan S. Cole, *Report on Northampton, Bucks. and Beds. Lace-Making,* 1891,
     Department of Science and Art (1892).
56. *Art Journal,* N. S. XIII (1874), p. 131.
57. C. C. Channer and M. E. Roberts, *Lace-Making in the Midlands* (1900),
     pp. 53—7, 73—5;
     North Bucks. Lace Association Pamphlet, n.d.
58. *Art Journal* (1896), pp. 297—302.
59. Lord Ernle (Rowland Edmund Prothero, Baron Ernle), *Whippingham to
     Westminster* (London, 1938).
60. Bedfordshire Lace Education Committee Minutes, 1907—24;
     Elementary Education Sub-Committee Report, 1930.
61. Beds. County Record Office, BY 9/3, October 1876.
62. M. Greenshields, 'A Survey of Lacemaking in Bedfordshire' (1955), MS.,
     Cecil Higgins Art Gallery, Bedford.
63. H.G. Tibbutt, *The Bunyan Meeting, Bedford, 1650—1973* (Bedford, n.d.),
     p. 121.
64. Beds. County Record Office, Z 6.
65. Beds. County Record Office, Bor. BP 189/1—2.
66. Probate Register, 29 January 1910.

Population figures from the Census Returns: 1841, PP (1844), XXVII; 1851, PP
(1852—3), LXXXVIII; 1861, PP (1863), LIII; 1871, PP (1873), LXXI; 1881,
LXXX; 1891, PP (1893—4), CVI.

Directory information except where a special reference is given from:
Pigot's London and Provincial New Commercial Directory, 1823—4.
Pigot's National Commercial Directory, 1830—1.
Pigot's & Company's Royal National and Commercial Directory and Topography,
1939.
Slater's Royal National and Commercial and Topographical Directory, 1850—1.
Craven and Company's Commercial Directory for the County of Bedford, 1853.
Post Office Directory, later Kelly's Post Office Directory, 1847—1930.

Select Bibliography

Buck, A., 'Middlemen in the Bedfordshire Lace Industry', *Bedfordshire Historical Record Society*, LVII (1978), 31—58

  'The Teaching of Lacemaking in the East Midlands', *Folk Life,* IV (1966), 39—50

Bury Palliser, F., *History of Lace,* London, 1864; 2nd edition, London, 1869; 3rd edition, London, 1875; revised edition by M. Jourdain and A. Dryden, London, 1902; reprint, Wakefield, 1976

Channer, C. C., *Practical Lacemaking. Bucks Point-Ground*, Leicester, 1928

Channer, C. C., and M. E. Roberts, *Lace-making in the Midlands, past and present,* London, 1900

Felkin, W., *History of Machine-wrought Hosiery and Lace,* London, 1867: reprint, Newton Abbot, 1967

Fitzrandolph, H. E., and M. D. Hay, *The Rural Industries of England and Wales*, III, Oxford, 1927

Freeman, C. E., *Pillow Lace in the East Midlands,* Luton Museum and Art Gallery, 1958

Halls, Z., *Machine-made Lace*, Nottingham City Art Gallery and Museum, 1964

Horn, P. L. R., 'Pillow Lacemaking in Victorian England: the Experience of Oxfordshire', *Textile History,* III (1972), 100—15

Spenceley, G. F. R., 'The Health and Discipline of Children in the Pillow Lace Industry in the Nineteenth Century', *Textile History,* VII (1976), 154—71

  'The Lace Associations: Philanthropic Movements to Preserve the Production of Hand-made Lace in Late Victorian and Edwardian England', *Victorian Studies,* XVI (1973), 433—52

Wardle, P., *Victorian Lace,* London, 1968

Wright, T., *The Romance of the Lace Pillow*, Olney, 1919; 2nd edition, 1924: reprint, London, 1971

Index

Abbot, John 13
Abington Pigotts 6
Abraham, Geo.,(Designer) 42
Adelaide, Queen 7
America 74; Civil War 74
Ampthill 14, 75, 88, 98
Art Journal 41, 87, 100
Astcote 12

Bagshawe, T. W. 15
Baptist Church (Bunyan Meeting) 6, 14, 87, 101–2
Batchelor, Thos. 4
Bedford 3, 6, 9, 10, 12–13, 14, 15, 39, 41, 44, 88, 102
    Bedford Bee 89; Cecil Higgins Art Gallery 15, 38,
        41, 42; Corporation 15; Library 15;
        Museum 15, 38
Bedfordshire 1, 9, 15, 37, 39, 44, 72, 86, 100, 101
Biddle, D. 40
Buckingham 40, 73, 85; Duke of B. 7
Buckinghamshire 1, 4, 44, 72, 76, 86, 100, 101
Bobbins 11, 12–13, 89; spangles 12–13; bobbin
        winder 11
Brackley 10
Broughton 74
Bruce-Clarke, E. 100
Burns, Maj. 10

Carnes, A. A. 38
Channer, C. C. 15–16, 37, 38
Chellington 14
Chesham 4
Cole, A. S. 99
Copestake, Moore Crampton & Co. 40
Cranfield 37, 88

Debenham & Freebody 41, 44
Design Act, 1842 8
Devonshire 1, 2, 72
Dress 1–2, 6–7, 14–15, 38–41, 100
    Bonnet veils 14; Caps 2, 6, 7, 38, 43–44, 70,
        71; Chemisettes 7; Cloaks 2; Collars 7,
        14, 39, 43, 44, 70, 72, 89–90; Cuffs 7, 39,
        43, 44, 69; Fans 41; Handkerchiefs 38,
        42–43, 44, 71; Lappets 39–40, 43, 69;
        Mantles 40; Parasols 41; Plastron 88;
        Scarves 2; Shawls 8, 39, 40; Ties 40;
        Undersleeves 7; Veils 14
Duties on lace 1, 9

Eaton Socon 74, 85
Education Act, 1870 98
Elstow 76, 85
Embroidery
    Berlin woolwork 71, 87, 101; Embroidered net 2,
        7, 38; whitework 71

Ernle, Lord 100
Exhibitions
    The Exhibition of the Works of Industry of all
        Nations (The Great Exhibition), 1851 39, 40,
        42–43, 44; The London International
        Exhibition, 1862 40–41, 43, 44, 70, 72; The
        Paris International Exhibition, 1867 8, 43,
        44, 70, 99; The Vienna Universal Exhibition,
        1873 43, 70, 87; The International Exhi-
        bition, London, 1874 43, 70, 87, 100;
        Northampton, 1891 99–100; The Chicago
        Exhibition, 1893 42–43, 89, 90

Factory Acts 72
Felmersham 90
Fox, Eliz., see Lester, Eliz.; Hannah 6; James 6

Goldington 14, 90, 102
Great Barford 88

Harrold 3, 38, 88
Haskins family 12
Hayward & Co. 40
Heathcoat, J. 2
High Wycombe 41, 73
Howell & James 41, 87

Keep Wm. 10
Kempston 14, 88
Keysoe 90
Kimbolton 102

Lace, East Midlands passim; Black silk lace 6–7, 39,
        40, 44, 73, 76, 86
    Alençon 101, Antwerp 1, 2; Bayeux 6; Blonde
        6–7, 38; Brussels 1, *point de gaze* 100; Caen
        6; Chantilly 2, 6, 40, 100; Cluny 88; Devon
        (Honiton) 8, 14, 37, 41, 44, 71, 72, 74, 87,
        89; Genoa 1, 40; Lille 1, 2, 16, 69; Maltese
        40–41, 42, 74, 88; Mechlin 1, 2, 39; Milan
        1, 69; Nottingham (machine net and lace) 2,
        7, 9, 14, 41, 72, 74, 88, 89; Torchon 89;
        Yak 89
Lace Associations 38, 99–101, 102
Lace dealers, manufacturers, merchants 1–3, 6–9,
        38–39, 72–73, 74
    Abrahams, S. 14, 42; Allen, Mrs 73, 76;
        Ayres Wm. 39, 73, 74; Biss, John, Wm. 73;
        Bithrey, Wm. 14; Braggins, A. 88; Cardwell,
        C. & T. 39, 41; Clarke, J. 37, 42; Clarke, S.
        14, 42; Coleman, J. 3; Collier, J. 14;
        Coombs, T. 88; Driver, Eliz. 15, 101–102;
        Gasking, J. 88; Gilbert, T. 41, 73; Godfroy,
        E. 40; Griffin, R. 3; Haines, Florence, 15–16,
        38, 70, 101, 102; Handscomb, W.H. 9, 37;

Harker, Mr 88; Haynes, T. 14; Hill, B. 39;
Hornsey, J. 41, 88; Marshall, Wm. 69, 73, 76;
Millward, James 7−9, 70, John 37, 40;
Mobbs, Mrs 74; Paine, Geo. 14; Peers, Sarah
14; Rabans Mr 88; Roberson, J. 37; Rose, E.P.
88; Sargeant, J. 41, 42; Savage, Miss 88;
Sim, C. J. 39; Smith, Geo. 37; Spencer, J. 16;
Thorp, R. 14; Viccars, R. 39, 41; Vincent, S.
39; Wilkins, Martha 14; Wright, Mrs 73
Lace dealers' sample books 16
Lace dealer's work book 38
Lace design 3, 7−9, 16, 37, 39−44, 69−72, 99−101
Lacemakers
    Armstrong, Mrs. 89, 90; Bayley, Emma, 75;
    Bowyer, Mrs 88; Cave, Mr 88, Mrs 99; Cox,
    Mrs 75; Curtis, Mrs 101, Catherine 10;
    Dawson, Mrs 4n., 88, 89, 99; Draper, Mrs 88;
    Emerson, Eliz. 76, Charlotte, 76; Freeman,
    Ann 10; Frewen, Eliz. 39; Godfrey, Zillah 10;
    Goodman, Mrs 76, 85; Harris, Mrs 75, Jane,
    75; Hulatt, Mrs 88; Jennings, Eliz. 10;
    Langley, Mrs 99; Pettit, Mrs 88; Read, Lucy
    75; Rose, Eliz. 39; Sansom, Miss 44; Swannell,
    Mrs 89, 90; Watts, Sarah 10; Webb, Mrs 88,
    98; Wood, Dinah 76; Wordsworth, Eliz. 75,
    76
    Earnings and hours of work 3−6, 9−10, 11, 74,
    75−76, 85−86, 89, 90, 98, 99; truck pay-
    ment 73, 74, 76, 85−86
    Numbers employed 3, 7, 9, 10, 72−73, 86, 90
Lace schools 4−5, 10, 72, 74−76, 85−86, 90,
    98−99
Lace stitches
    Clothwork 16, 37, 42, 43, 69, 72, 90; half-
    stitch clothwork 43
    Gimp (cordonnet) 11, 16, 37, 38, 42, 69, 87
    Grounds, mesh (point ground) 2, 15−16, 37−38,
    40, 41−42, 69−70; bars 38, 40, 42, 43, 69,
    72; plaited ground 41−42, 70, 74
    Picots (purls) 42, 43, 44, 69, 70, 90
    Plaits, tallies 41−42, 43, 69, 70, 72, 90
    Point raccroc (joining stitch) 40
    Raised work 69
Landseer, Sir Edwin 72
Lester, Thomas (Thomazin) 1, 6, 14, 16, 37−43,
    44, 69−72, 74−75, 85−88, 98−99, 102;
    Eliz. (Fox) 6, 14, 37, 87; Charles Fox 14,
    70−72, 87−89, 101; Thomas James 13−16,
    70−72, 87−89, 102; Eliz. Sophia 14, 87, 102;
    Sarah 14, 87; Amy 15,42
Lidlington 4
London 3, 37, 100
Lumbis, Geo. 13
Luton Museum 15−16, 37, 38, 42, 69, 89

Marlow 39
Marston Moretaine 74
Matthiason, J. H. 9
Maulden 75

Newport Pagnell 9, 39, 69, 73, 74, 75, 76
Northampton 38, 39, 41, 99, 100; N. Museum 88
Northamptonshire 1, 4n., 15, 38, 44, 72, 86
Nottingham 8, 9, 41, 88

Oakley 100
Odell 98
Olney 1, 7, 16, 37, 39, 40
Oxfordshire 73

Padbury 39, 41
Palliser, Mrs Bury 87−88, 89
Pattern drafts 3, 7−8, 15, 16, 37−38, 43, 70
Patterns (parchments, cards) 3, 7−8, 11, 16,
    38, 43, 73, 85, 100, 101
Paulerspury 39
Pillows 10−11; pillow-horses 10−11
Pins 11
Prestwood 73
Pytchley 75

The Queen 44, 88

Radwell 88
Renhold 13, 37
Ridgmont 99
Riseley 88
Roxton 88
Rudge, Bradford 70
Ruskin, J. 71

Sandy 41
Sharnbrook 14
Stevington 88; Baptist Church 37
Stony Stratford 10, 85
Straw plaiting 9, 75, 98

Tempsford 37
Terry, Mrs 42
Thread (linen) 7, 9, 11, 12, 73, 99; silk 6, 9, 73,
    74, 76, 86, 99; cotton 9, 11, 12, 76; worsted
    89
Thurleigh 89, 90
Treadwin, Mrs 8, 87
Trevelyan, Lady 44, 71
Turvey 14, 37, 39, 88

Usher, J. 102

Victoria, Queen 44
Victoria and Albert Museum 44

Wellingborough 10, 16
White, J. 75, 76
Wilden 88, 99
Willington 88, 99
Wilshampstead, Wilstead 37, 75
Wooding, Jos. 38
Wootton 37
Workshops Act, 1867 90, 98
Wynne, Eugenia 2

Young, Arthur 4